Cataloguing in Publication Data

Gillham, John 1947-
Peaks of the Yorkshire Dales : a hillwalkers' companion,
1 Hill walking. North Yorkshire (England)
I Title II Iddon, Phil 1954-
914.28404859

ISBN 0-9515996-1-5

PEAKS of the YORKSHIRE DALES
A Hillwalkers' Companion

by John Gillham & Phil Iddon

Grey Stone Books
Hoddlesden

JOHN GILLHAM was born in 1947 in Bournemouth. He has lived in
Lancashire for most of his life, building up a detailed knowledge of the
Pennine Hills. After many years at British Aerospace, he is now a full-time
writer/photographer and publisher.

PHIL IDDON was born in Chorley in 1954. He has a degree in Mechanical
Engineering and works as a senior engineer with British Aerospace at Preston.
He began mountain walking in 1977 and particularly favours the French Alps
and Scottish Mountains. He is married and lives in the Ribble Valley.

ACKNOWLEDGEMENTS: We would like to thank those who have helped
with the production of this book; our wives Nicola and Sheila, who have
tramped the hills on forays in less than good weather; Edgar Gillham for his
editorial assistance; Ken Vickers for the book title; the willing staff of Preston
and Clitheroe Tourist Offices for their assistance with the accommodation and
last but not least, Colin Straker, National Park Warden at Grassington for his
advice on the route around Conistone.

Phil Iddon wrote and photographed the Three Peaks section and part of the
Howgill Fells section. The remainder was written and photographed by John
Gillham. Drawings and sketches are also by John Gillham.

Cover Photographs: Pen-y-Ghent from the south. Rear: Looking west from
the edge of Ingleborough's summit to the Irish Sea. Both by Phil Iddon.

ALSO BY THE SAME AUTHORS

"Bowland & the South Pennines" Grey Stone Books

AND BY JOHN GILLHAM

"Snowdonia to the Gower" Diadem Books

CONTENTS

THE YORKSHIRE DALES

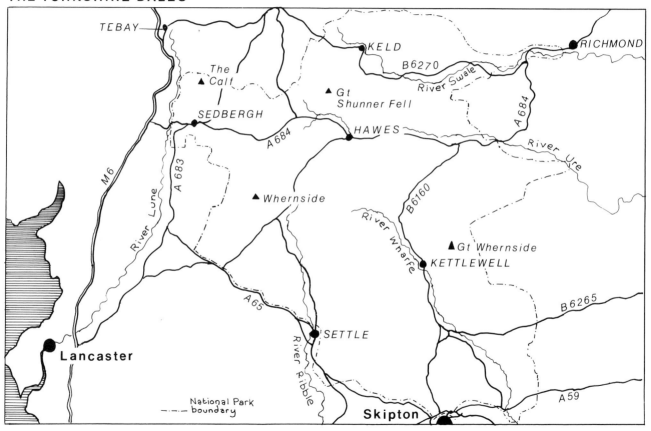

INTRODUCTION

I first came upon the Yorkshire Dales in 1977 when taking a spin in the silver Lancia coupé that I had just bought. I had yet to discover the joys of mountain walking and a trip to the country usually involved a short stroll followed by a pub lunch and tour of the local shops. The Lancia behaved well - probably the last time it ever did! The weather did not. It poured down all day. Clinging clouds and mirk hung on the hillslopes rendering them lifeless or so it seemed to the uninitiated.

I returned a few years later as a walker on the Pennine Way. It still rained and, as I strode over Pen-y-Ghent with only the ground under my feet visible, I remembered 1977. But strangely, through the silver mist I could sense the heartbeat of the moor: through the embracing damp air I could inhale the aroma of peat, heather and grass and through the eery silence the calls of the curlew, plover and lark could be heard.

The Yorkshire Dales National Park covers 680 square miles of Pennine Upland Country between the Lune Valley and the Vale of York. For the masses who flock to its tourist honeypots, the park is synonymous with cultivated rural charm - a land of tree-lined becks, sleepy picturesque villages and dry-stone wall mosaics etched onto verdant, flower-decked pastures and limestone escarpments. *Peaks of the Yorkshire Dales* sets out to explore a different world however - one of high, wild and windswept summits. They may not be as imposing as their Lakeland neighbours but the Yorkshire

Peaks do have a more subtle appeal - those who seek only grandeur will be blind to subtlety.

Each mountain has its own special character and charm. Majestic Ingleborough soars from its tiered limestone platform in proud, sweeping scree-strewn arcs whilst Whernside, gentle giant that it is, rises gradually like a whale from the ocean. If Ingleborough is King of the Dales then Pen-y-Ghent is surely Crown Prince for its imposing mountain architecture rules Ribblesdale.

Those who do not like to share their hills with the masses will love Calf Top Gragareth and Great Coum. Close to Yorkshire's borders with Lancashire and Cumbria, these outliers have never had the popularity they deserve. To their north are the Howgill Fells, sleek silurian hills, strangely bereft of walls to distort or accentuate their contours. Cut by steep-sided, wild and uninhabited valleys, they offer the fell-walker the opportunity to stride out with a freedom to roam seldom found elsewhere in England.

The Northern and Eastern Peaks are more sombre places - partially the preserve of the grouse-shooting men. Heather clad expanses, a blaze of purple in summer, recede to dark, peat-hagged quagmires of the watersheds. This is tough walking country but summits like Lovely Seat and Baugh Fell are rewarding for those who like solitude and space.

Phil and I have devised thirty day walks (mainly circular). None is too demanding for the averagely fit person, but the knowledge of how to use map and compass is essential. My sketches are in no way intended to substitute for proper Ordnance Survey Maps. At the start of each chapter the relevant map numbers are listed - both 1;50000 Landranger and 1:25000 Outdoor Leisure. The latter are strongly recommended for they plot the field boundaries so helpful to route finding in the lower dales.

John Gillham, Darwen 1991

Ingleborough, Whernside and Pen-y-Ghent, known collectively as the Three Peaks, have suffered badly from erosion and yet, how can you exclude what is arguably the most spectacular mountain walking in the whole of the Yorkshire Dales? In short you cannot.

In my opinion the erosion can be attributed largely to the Three Peaks Walk - a twenty-six mile challenge which is undertaken each year by thousands of people not only on foot but on cycles. Some raise money for charity, others purely test their stamina. Their objectives may be admirable but surely these magnificent fells should be saved for those who fully appreciate them and not used as an oversized obstacle course.

In the book John and I have tried to describe less popular walks and summits for we both firmly believe that a greater awareness of alternatives will lead to less stress on the more popular places.

One of my most cherished memories of the Yorkshire Peaks was crystallised on a January day when the country was gripped by a spell of Siberian weather. Undeterred by forecasts of extreme sub-zero temperatures, I made an enthusiastic start to the ascent of Ingleborough. The atmospheric conditions were magnificent and everything adorned with ice crystals, which glistened in the glancing light of the winter sun. Toy-like figures in brightly coloured cagoules diverted my gaze towards the summit massif and, in a bouyant mood, I covered ground quickly with frozen snow crunching noisily underfoot.

On reaching the summit plateau, I was surprisingly alone. By now the sun was low in the sky, glowing blood red and sinking fast through an icy mist. I was suddenly struck by the solitude and became increasingly aware of the hostile conditions! The wind, now stronger, swirled furiously between the summit cairns and I became a stranger to the land - seemingly guilty of trespass. My earlier euphoria was replaced by a nervous feeling of remoteness and vulnerability. In this mood I left the summit with the hard, wind-blown snow stinging my face. My pace quickened to escape the mountain's ire. What had begun as a pleasant and familiar hill walk had transpired into an epic - one which stays fresh in the mind and would not be traded for a score of sunny summer walks however grand the scenery.

Phil Iddon, Wilpshire 1991

MOUNTAINS OF THE YORKSHIRE DALES

Mountain	Height ft	Height M	Section	route
Whernside	2419ft	736m	3 Peaks	17-19
Ingleborough	2372	723	"	13-16
Great Shunner Fell	2340	716	Northern	3
Wild Boar Fell	2324	708	"	2
Great Whernside	2310	704	Eastern	9
Buckden Pike	2302	702	"	10-11
Pen-y-Ghent	2277	694	3 Peaks	20-22
Great Coum	2250	687	Western	23-25
Swarth Fell	2235	681	Northern	3
The Calf	2220	676	Howgills	6 & 8
The Calders	2213	674	"	6
Baugh Fell	2216	678	Northern	1
Lovely Seat	2213	675	"	3
Rogan's Seat	2203	672	"	4
Fountains Fell	2191	668	Southern	30-31
Dodd Fell	2190	668	Northern	5
Great Dummacks	2160	659	Howgills	6
Yarlside	2097	639	"	7
Fell Head	2070	623	"	8
Gragareth	2058	627	Western	25-26
Wether Fell	2015	614	Northern	5
Rye Loaf Hill	1794	547	Southern	29
Kensgriff	1790	545	Howgills	7
Greets Hill	1676	508		*
Cracoe Fell	1660	505	Eastern	12

The precipitous eastern edge of Wild Boar Fell (route 2)

THE NORTHERN PEAKS

BAUGH FELL

Route 1 Circular from Rawthey Bridge

WILD BOAR FELL

Route 2 Circular from the Eden Valley

GREAT SHUNNER FELL/LOVELY SEAT

Route 3 Circular from Hawes

ROGAN'S SEAT

Route 4 Circular from Keld

DODD FELL & WETHER FELL

Route 5 Circular from Gayle

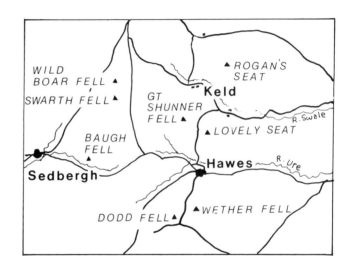

ADDITIONAL INFORMATION

O.S. Landranger Maps 1:50000 Nos 98 'Wensleydale and Upper Wharfedale'; 91 'Appleby in Westmorland Area' (for Rogan's Seat) and 97 'Kendal to Morecambe' (for Fell End)
O.S. Outdoor Leisure 1:25000 N0 30 (Yorkshire Dales North & Central)

ACCOMODATION

Stone House Hotel, Sedbusk (north of Hawes) (09697.571); The Green Dragon Inn, Hardraw (Hawes) (0969.667392); Cocketts Hotel, Hawes (0969.667312); The Kearton Guest House, Thwaite (Swaledale) (0748.86277); and the highest pub in England, 'The Tan Hill Inn' north of Keld (0833.28246). Youth Hostels at Hawes (0969.667368), Keld (0748.86259) & Kirkby Stephen (07683.71793)
Camp-sites at Keld; Usha Gap, Muker; Bainbridge Ings, Hawes & Brown Moor Farm, Hawes (0969.667338)

Railway Stations at Darlington (for buses to Richmond then on to Dales) and Kirkby Stephen

BAUGH FELL

Lying across the lush green Rawthey Valley from the steep-sided and shapely Howgills is Baugh (pronounced Bo) Fell. From the valley floor this sprawling hill seems uninspiring when compared to its near neighbours. Not to put too fine a point on it, it is a big fat lump. Do not let outward appearances put you off for the ascent of this lump is most worthwhile and studded with precious jewels - waterfalls, a multitude of wildlife and spectacular panoramas from its wide and airy summit.

Baugh Fell is separated from its neighbour Swarth Fell by the beautiful but seldom frequented valleys of Grisedale and Uldale whilst, to the south, its unrelentingly steep flanks decline into Garsdale. The vast 'U' shaped plateau swells to the summit of Knoutberry Haw, 2216 feet above sea level and is dissected by Rawthey Gill which drains the tarns on East Baugh Fell. To the north, high above the Rawthey Valley is West Baugh Fell Tarn. This wild and isolated place is a barometer for the mood of the heavens. On a clear, calm and sunny day, when the waters are saturated with the blue from the skies, you can look across to the shapely Howgill Fells and the sheer tranquil beauty of the place is laid out for all to see. When the clouds hang dark and low, concealing the fell-tops, this sombre sheet lies restless and unfriendly, amidst the colourless, wind-thrashed moor grass.

Approaches to the summit are generally limited to the western side, although there is one good route from Garsdale Head via Grisedale and its Pike. Those from the south are made unsuitable by lack of access through the farmlands of Garsdale. Whichever route you chose, save Baugh Fell for a fine weather ascent and you will be rewarded with a memorable day.

Route 1
BAUGH FELL - A Circular from Rawthey Bridge

Distance 10 Miles - fairly strenuous

Rawthey Bridge lies in a verdant niche between high hills. Here the Sedbergh - Kirkby Stephen road crosses the River Rawthey, which leaves mainstream civilization and heads south eastwards for the hills. The Rawthey in fact has its source close to Baugh Fell's summit (Knoutberry Haw). Its wild and romantic valley is from here on known as Uldale and will guide us to Baugh Fell's heartlands.

There is ample car-parking space by the bridge (ref.713978) and the start of the route is marked with a signpost. The way follows an old drovers' road. The grooved track winds up the lower slopes of Bluecaster before being abandoned at a reedy hollow for another track which heads eastwards across empty moorland high above the river. The bleak pale slopes of Wild Boar and Swarth Fells swell to the horizon above the copses and pastures of Uldale and dominate views ahead. After passing the ruins of an old lime kiln, the route descends to the riverbank. Here the Rawthey cascades in a series of cataracts through a sylvan glen. The sketchy,

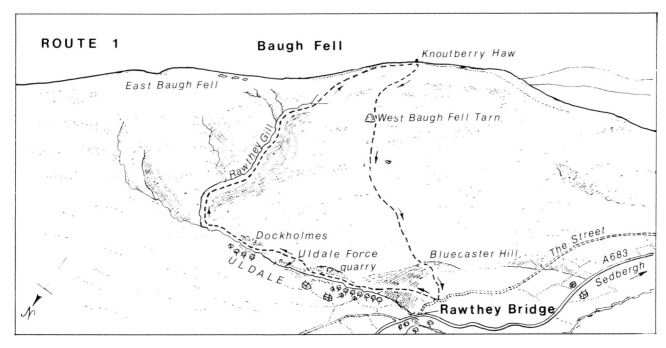

ROUTE 1   Baugh Fell

riverside path now continues, passing more waterfalls. Limestone cliffs have been quarried and hereabouts the path is rough. Beyond the quarry, opposite the impressive cascade of one of the Rawthey's feeder streams, it becomes necessary to climb away from the river. The reason for this becomes evident upstream as Uldale Force comes into view. The waterfall's powerful foam tumbles over a nick in tall stratified cliffs into a pool below. In fact these dark, mossy precipices bar all exits from the gorge. Do not approach the falls too closely for the shaly slopes are very unstable and dangerous.

Beyond Uldale Force, the intermittent track leads to the riverbank once more and passes through Dockholmes, a shallow tree-fringed limestone gorge. Further upstream a wilder world of high bare moorlands at the head of Grisedale is entered. Here the Rawthey's ravine veers to the right. It is traced on a winding course upwards to Baugh Fell. The river is still boisterous and displays many waterfalls. Beyond the highest of these, the gill opens out. By following the western tributary the course will lead to Baugh Fell's summit, Knoutberry Haw. This is marked by a stone trig point close to a dry-stone wall which straddles the ridge from east to west. From here you can look across verdant Garsdale over Rise Hill to Great Coum, Whernside and Pen-y-Ghent. The Howgills can be seen end to end on the western horizon with Wild Boar and Swarth Fell completing the panorama to the north.

On the return route follow the wide ridge northwards passing West Baugh Fell Tarn before veering north westwards high above the strath of the River Rawthey. On the declining slopes of West Baugh Fell and Raven Thorn the terrain is more marshy - the tussocky grass of the higher ground giving way to mosses and reeds.

The descent is fairly easy however and made more pleasing by the wide views of the Howgills. Cautley Crag and its adjacent waterfalls look particularly spectacular, flanked by the steep-sloped dome-backed Yarlside.

Between Raven Thorn and Bluecaster is a slight depression. Pale outcrops and shake-holes give evidence of the transition to limestone country. The mosses are replaced by the grasses of Bluecaster which is then scaled before descending to meet the old drovers' road which was encountered at the beginning of the day. This will lead once more to the road at Rawthey Bridge.

Uldale Force

WILD BOAR FELL

Wild Boar Fell has two faces. From Mallerstang in the Eden Valley, it is characterised by dark gritstone cliffs which thrust from a moorland plinth of limestone and shales. Its eastern flanks are gentler - even some of the names such as Fell End Clouds suggest an amiable nature.

    Wild Boar has much to offer the walker - hidden waterfalls, crags, cliffs and marvellous views over Yorkshire and Cumbria. Those who climb to its top will not be disappointed.

Route 2
WILD BOAR FELL - A Circular from the Eden Valley

Distance 8¹/₂ miles - moderate

Cars can be parked by an old quarry by Far Cote Gill (ref.773968) on the B6259 Garsdale to Kirkby Stephen Road in the Eden Valley. Here the dark cliffs of Mallerstang Edge on the right hand side face those of Wild Boar on the left. The splendid route begins with a short road walk northwards to Aisgill Farm. Opposite to the farm, the hillwalk proper begins on a path which passes under the arches of a railway viaduct. By staying close to the stream (Aisgill), the spout-like waterfalls of Low White Kirk can be seen. A detour can be made upstream to see those of White Kirk but footsteps will have to be retraced.

Swarth Fell from Wild Boar Fell

    Beyond White Kirk grassy fellsides are traversed northwards to reach a dry stone wall which is followed until it bends right. Here the route continues NNW along a line of shakeholes, potholes (the Angerholme Pots) and limestone clints with the exciting dark gritstone crags of Wild Boar to the left. A sketchy path then rakes up the hillsides aiming for a col to the north of the Nab.

The col is marked by the intersection of a fence and a dry-stone wall corner. From here the edge is traced, climbing southwards to the Nab itself. Views along the line of the sombre cliffs are spectacular as are those westwards to the shapely Howgills. In eastern vistas, Mallerstang Edge forms a bold front to waves of peaty hills rising to the massif of Great

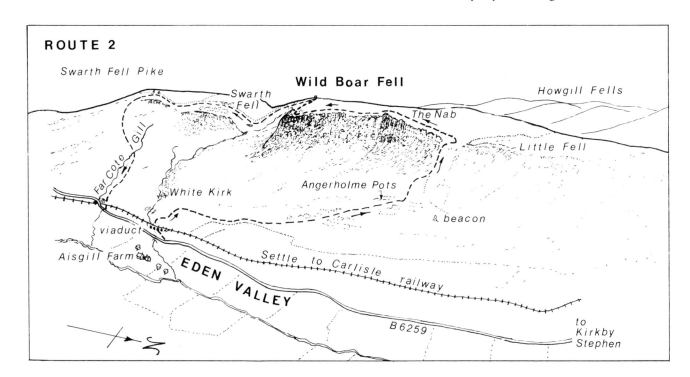

The Nab, Wild Boar Fell from near the Angerholme Po

Shunner Fell. If you are lucky you may see a steam train struggling up the gradients of the Eden Valley on the famous Settle to Carlisle Line.

The route continus along the edge to its highest point, adorned with several stone men (cairns). This is probably the best place en route for a lunch stop for there is adequate shelter from the elements and the views are still good. The true summit of Wild Boar lies north west. Marked by a stone shelter and trig point, its views are inferior, the valleys being obscured by the vast plateau. A summit is a summit however and it has to be visited and thus a north westerly course is set to reach it before turning south west on a declining spur to the col beneath Swarth Fell, the next objective. Cairns mark the route at the southern end of the plateau. The peaty col, which houses a small tarn, can be marshy after rain. It is a fairly simple climb to Swarth Fell and a nearby stone wall would be a guide in misty conditions. The summit has pleasant views down the lonely Uldale Valley. Continuing along the ridge, the next summit is the slightly lower Swarth Fell Pike. The descent is trackless initially. It begins north eastwards to reach Far Cote Gill. The north banks of this little stream are then traced all the way to the starting point by the quarry.

GREAT SHUNNER FELL & LOVELY SEAT

Great Shunner is the highest point of a sprawling, peat-hagged massif between Wensleydale and Swaledale. The mountain is a colossal frump with few features worthy of note and its peaty slopes have, in places, been eroded by Pennine Wayers into quagmires. Despite all this, Great Shunner has a certain charm. Outside the summer months it is not overcrowded and offers wide views over surrounding peaks - those of Wensleydale and Swaledale are sublime and not to be missed.

Lovely Seat lies across the Buttertubs Pass from Great Shunner. Although the summit is similar in nature it shows a fairer facade to Wensleydale in the form of the tiered limestone cliffs of its southern outlier, Pike Hill.

Route 3
GREAT SHUNNER FELL & LOVELY SEAT - a circular from Hawes

Distance 14 miles - hard going and long

Hawes is a busy market town situated on the southern edge of the wide Wensleydale Valley. It is surrounded by high hills with impressive ivory-cragged terraces. The loftiest of the hills at 2340 feet (716m) is Great Shunner Fell. One of the most satisfying long walks combines this giant with its neighbour, Lovely Seat.

After taking the Hardraw road out of the village to a point just north of the disused railway, we use the official Pennine Way route, which follows a path across fields to the left. In fact it just cuts a corner and rejoins the road a little short of twin-arched Haylands Bridge (876904) spanning the River Ure. The bridge is crossed and, a short way on, another

Descending Swarth Fell

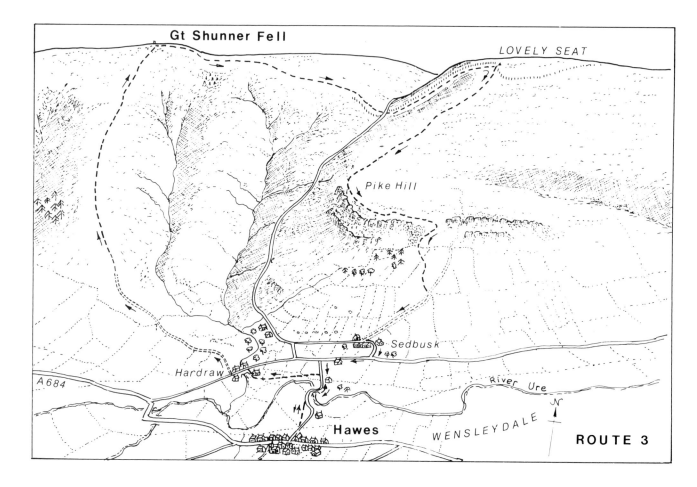

Gt Shunner Fell

LOVELY SEAT

Pike Hill

Sedbusk

River Ure

Hardraw

A684

Hawes

WENSLEYDALE

ROUTE 3

Pennine Way signpost advises us to traverse more lowland pastures westwards towards Hardraw.

At the back of the Green Dragon Inn is England's highest waterfall, Hardraw Force. It is a spectacle not to be missed. To view it you will have to pass through the inn and pay a nominal toll. Unexpectedly, prior to reaching the waterfall, a circular stone bandstand is encountered. It is the setting for the popular annual Hardraw Force Brass Band Competition and entries come from bands all over Yorkshire. The force is really impressive, especially after heavy rains. It cascades ninety-six feet in one step over tree-fringed limestone crags to a dark pool below. In 1890, after disastrous floods, the lip of Hardraw force was destroyed allowing the river to alter course and rush down to the base in a series of cascades. The landowner, Lord Wharncliffe then instigated the reconstruction of the lip in order to restore the falls to their former glory.

Beyond Hardraw a track bound by dry-stone walls is used on the long trek up the massive moorland expanses of Great Shunner Fell. Initially the route is interesting and easy-paced with good retrospective views of Hawes and Wensleydale. (Later Ingleborough peeps over the shoulder of Widdale Fell). When the open fellsides are reached the walk loses some of its appeal. It is a long way to the summit and little changes, for Great Shunner's concave slopes conceal the summit mass until the very end. In some parts the slopes are eroded and the brown gooey peat breaks through grassy slopes in haggs becoming more frequent as height is gained. Many cairns line the route and offer useful guidance in misty conditions.

Reaching the summit lifts the spirits for it is as good a viewpoint as any in the Dales. The Northern Pennines from Mickle Fell to Cross Fell are revealed behind the dusky moorland spread of Nine Standards Rigg. In southern panoramas the Three Peaks of Yorkshire, Pen-y-Ghent, Ingleborough and Whernside all figure on the horizon rising above lower and less distinctive fells. Looking to the west over neighbouring peak Ure Head are the fells of Lakeland. In the opposite direction is Lovely Seat, our next objective. Lying between is the trackless terrain of Thwaite Common.

Instead of following the broad Pennine Way to Swaledale, a traverse of rough moors eastwards to Little Shunner is made. A south easterly course is then taken across the watershed between Fossdale Gill and Grainy Gill to the Buttertubs Pass. Here the Hawes to Thwaite road straddles the lonely desolate moorland.

The ascent to Lovely Seat is a simple one, following the fence all the way to the summit, passing close to some stone cairns en route. From the summit it is interesting to look back to Great Shunner Fell, which appears as the sprawling giant it truly is!

The return route to Hawes is initially trackless. After rainy periods the going across peat haggs can be quite rough but those who are familiar with Pennine hills will find this nothing out of the ordinary. The best course is to descent SSW, parallel to the road. In the later stages tall cairns will lead to the right of way on the limestone terrain of Pike Hill. Here a delightful track traces the craggy edge. When the right of way veers from the edge, it is abandoned. Our route continues immediately above the limestone crags and we are rewarded with superior views across Wensleydale. Hawes can be seen lying snugly beyond the lazy, meandering River Ure. To the south verdant meadows swell to the crags of Wether Fell whilst on the horizon is the unmistakable shapely peak of Ingleborough and that whaleback colossus of Whernside.

The right of way is rejoined by a gap in the crags (ref. 884923). It is followed southwards to a cart track which then declines over high pastures to meet Shutt Lane (ref. 888915). This walled track leads down to the high hamlet of Sedbusk. The return to Hawes, which lies one mile to the south, can be made using the country lanes.

Gt. Shunner Fell from Lovely Seat

ROGAN'S SEAT

There are no rights of way to the summit of Rogan's Seat but, being one of Yorkshire's higher peaks, it is often visited and routes are included in guide books. It should be noted, however that it is an active grouse moor and access is a delicate subject. Good behaviour by walkers would obviously aid relationships with landowners and gamekeepers.

Fellwalkers looking for quietude will probably enjoy Rogan's Seat. There is no summit to speak of - just a pile of stones on a vast heathery plateau. The silence, accentuated by the spasmodic cackle of red grouse or the cry of a golden plover, is truly golden. The mountain dips its feet in the River Swale at Keld to the south and is parcelled in the north by a high and wild moorland road where stands the highest inn in England at Tan Hill.

Route 4
ROGAN'S SEAT - A Circular from Keld via Tan Hill

Distance 12 miles - strenuous

Keld is a splendid hamlet - a place of which Wainwright once said that time was measured in centuries. Here a chapel and its congregation of stone cottages are set amongst high pastures beneath lofty wild moorland and overlooking the wooded glens of Upper Swaledale. Keld is known for its waterfalls. There are spaces for car parking in the village although its

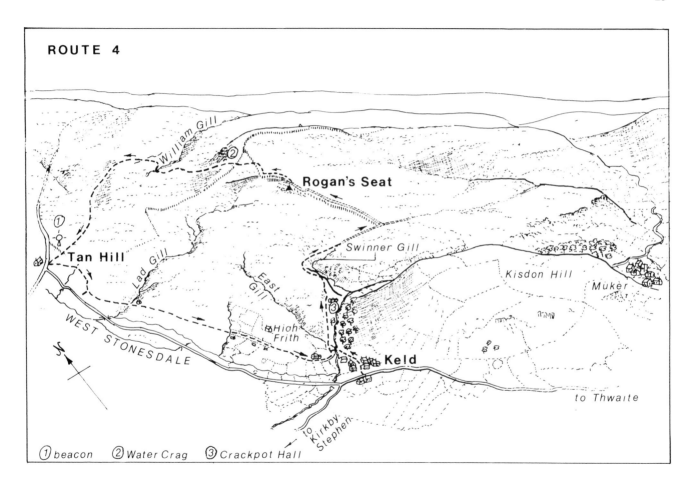

ROUTE 4

① beacon ② Water Crag ③ Crackpot Hall

popularity makes this problematic in the busy summer months.

This fine circular walk utilises parts of both Pennine Way and Coast to Coast long distance routes and takes in limestone ravines and high desolate tops studded with the interests of old lead and coal mines. It begins at the bottom of the village on a muddy track signposted 'to Kisdon Force'. After a couple of hundred yards a path descends to the left to cross a wooden bridge over the Swale. Here the lively river is confined by limestone cliffs and thick woodland. Close by is the impressive East Gill Force which tumbles from the hillsides to join the Swale. To the east of the waterfall the Pennine Way and Coast to Coast paths diverge. Our route follows the eastbound line of the Coast to Coast Path which climbs fellsides north of the Swale on a well defined, stony track. Thunderous sounds of numerous waterfalls echo in the sylvan valley below. The track is left just short of Crackpot Hall on a path with sketchy beginnings. This passes behind the impressive ruin. In a lovely view to the south, the Swale has changed to a southerly course, meandering between Kisdon Hill and Ivelet Moor. In the mid-distance it can be seen resuming a west-east course, flowing in a widening valley towards Richmond.

Beyond a gate a grassy path leads northwards high above the rocky ravine of Swinner Gill. It descends slightly to the extensive lead mines below Swinner Gill Kirk. From here a narrow track climbs by the northern banks of East Grain to reach the wild heather moors, where it joins a wide flinted track. At the highest point (ref.926012) this right of way is abandoned for a shooters' track which climbs NNW by a wire fence across the desolate grouse moors .

Swinner Gill in winter

The summit of Rogan's Seat 2204 ft (672m) is a modest affair, marked by a small stone cairn. Views are wide, if unspectacular. To the north the undulating moors lead the eye to Mickle Fell whilst the western prospect includes High Seat and Nine Standards Rigg. Great Shunner Fell and Lovely Seat dominate southern vistas but restrict distant views.

Although the shooters' track continues beyond the summit it is of no further use and a trackless course is taken NNE over rough heather moors to Water Crag. A new wire fence (not marked on maps at 1991) along the parish boundary will be of help in mist. From the 662 spot height (663 on 1:50000 maps) another fence (also marking parish boundaries) will be seen ahead (running westwards). Bear NNW towards the gate in this fence for it marks the position of Water Crag. (If mist prevails continue to the intersection of fences a couple of hundred yards further north east and double back to the same point.) From Water Crag descend northwards to-

wards the bridleway on Scollit Hill (approx. ref. 923055). The cairned track is then picked up and followed westwards into William Gill where a prominent path continues north eastwards. After a couple of hundred yards, close to an old ruin, a sketchy bridleway climbs out of the ravine to head north westwards, descending briefly to cross Lad Gill. The climb to Mirk Fell is helped by a few cairns which mark the route. The track which descends from the edge of Mirk Fell to Tan Hill is intermittent and sheep tracks confuse the issue. It is simpler to make a beeline for the distant radio transmitter beacon which lies just to the east of the Tan Hill Inn, making deviations only to avoid the rougher terrain.

The return route from Tan Hill to Keld is much easier

Tan Hill

and quicker than the outward journey so do not worry too much about the time. Just over two hours of light will see you home - less if you are a fast walker! The inn would make a good intermediate refreshment stop for those with time to spare. It is a great favourite amongst Pennine Way walkers and local farmers alike.

The route back to Keld follows the Pennine Way on a moorland track due south of the inn. It runs parallel to a lonely lane which straddles the high bleak moors before descending to Keld. A right fork is taken about half a mile south of the inn. After passing through an area of quarries and pits the path descends close to the road at Lad Gill (not the same one previously mentioned). It then climbs to the shoulders of Stonesdale Moor. Beyond a stone-built barn and gate, a walled track is followed beneath the stark dwelling of High Frith and past two more barns. As the rutted track climbs to Low Frith Farm it is abandoned. The route then continues southwards beneath Black Moor. By now the desolation has receded and, although the adjacent landscape is austere, rough pastures and hardy broad-leafed trees have replaced the heather moors close to the valley bottom. Ahead the shapely Kisdon Hill, which lies above Keld, can be seen.

In the very pleasant finale, the path enters into the verdant valley of the Swale, descending on a walled track and through the farmyard of East Stonesdale. From here the village of Keld can clearly be seen in its hollow beneath the high fells.

A walled track declines further to return to the splendid cascades of East Gill Force where steps are retraced across the Swale bridge to the village.

DODD FELL & WETHER FELL

Dodd Fell and Wether Fell lie on either side of Sleddale and are connected by a high saddle at its head. The saddle is scaled by a narrow lane linking Hawes and Buckden and both fells can be ascended quickly, if uneventfully, from here. Two more ancient roads straddle these fells - the West Cam Road and the Roman Cam High Road. The latter linked camps at Bainbridge and Ribblesdale.

Dodd Fell is the culmination of a whaleback ridge rising gently from the fields of Hawes in Wensleydale and declining in the south to the wilderness of Oughtershaw. Although it is outranked and outshone by neighbours Whernside and Pen-y-Ghent Dodd Fell does offer interesting views and different perspectives of more famous summits.

Wether Fell's slopes are more verdant and only on the very top does it possess that wild moorland atmosphere. As a viewpoint it is magnificent. On one side, across Wensleydale, is Great Shunner, High Seat and Wild Boar - on the other, beyond Raydale and lovely Semer Water, is the flat-topped Addleborough and, further afield, Buckden Pike.

Route 5
DODD FELL & WETHER FELL from Gayle

Distance 15 miles - strenuous

This long route follows two ancient mountain roads and visits two of the less popular but highly commendable peaks of

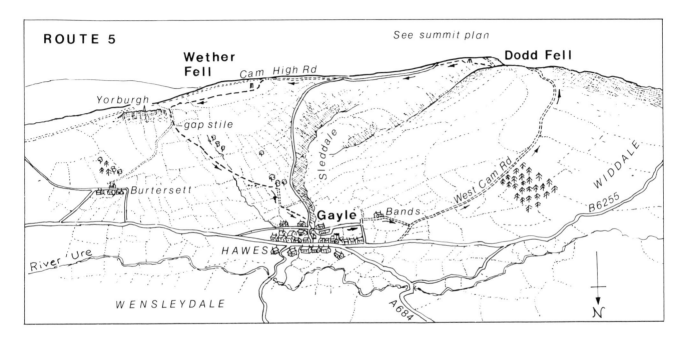

Yorkshire. Commencing at the bridge over Gayle Beck, the westbound lane is taken, passing the chapel and West End Farm (only named on 1:25000 Maps) to a tee junction (ref. 865891). After turning left here, a right turn is then made along Bands Lane. This passes The Bands (farm) and terminates at the Cam Road which climbs south westwards on the shoulders of a fellside known, perhaps unkindly, as Backsides. These rough pastures decline to wild and woolly Widdale. Northern views across Wensleydale are filled with the vast moorland expanses of Great Shunner Fell and Lovely Seat.

The track climbs steadily to pass a forestry plantation before reaching the Pennine Way route at Ten End. The steep, stark slopes of Widdale Fell to the west are now fully in view. A couple of isolated farmsteads and a spruce plantation do little to tame the wild landscape. The Cam Road is abandoned when the open moors are reached. A southbound course over rough ground will lead to the trig point crowning Dodd Fell's summit. Impressive include Ingleborough, Whernside and Pen-y-Ghent, standing proud of rolling ochre moorlands.

To avoid clambering over walls it is best to continue westwards from the summit to rejoin the Cam Road and the Pennine Way. This passes through an area of limestone clints and outcrops to reach a tarmac lane at Kidhow Gate where there are superb views over the desolate upper valley of Langstrothdale. The lane is followed eastwards before veering northwards to ref.862853 where it is abandoned for the Cam High Road. This ancient Roman highway, which would once have carried legions from forts at Chester to Carlisle via Bainbridge, leads north eastwards along Wether Fell's southern flanks. At ref 873865 the wall on the left hand side terminates leaving the walker free to climb northwards on open fell to the large cairn on the summit, which is known as Drumaldrace. This fine vantage point gives wide views over Wensleydale to the high hills. Wild Boar looks particularly attractive from this angle.

The descent from Wether Fell begins with a trek north eastwards over peat-hagged terrain to locate a gate in a drystone wall (ref.880875). From here a rutted track is met and followed to the western side of the craggy knoll of Yorburgh where it is left for a footpath descending north westwards across high meadows. The route, obscure in places, keeps to the right of a small wood and crosses Blackburn Sike to the north of these. At ref. 875887, on a grassy terrace, a well-defined path rakes down to another wood. Here a narrow walled track turns southwards to descend amongst colourful flower-covered meadows to Gayle.

OTHER ROUTES IN THE NORTHERN PEAKS

WILD BOAR & SWARTH FELL - A circular from Rawthey Bridge
Distance 12 miles - strenuous
Follow the path used to ascend Baugh Fell to the footbridge over Rawthey Gill (ref.727967) opposite Needle House. After crossing the bridge, climb out of the valley bottom by a drystone wall to a farm road which then leads past Uldale House. After fording a gill a footpath leaves the farm track and

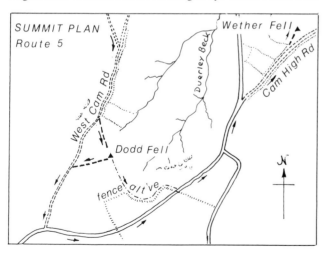

SUMMIT PLAN
Route 5

Wether Fell

Duerley Beck

West Cam Rd

Cam High Rd

Dodd Fell

fence alive

N

continues parallel to Rawthey Gill. Whin Stone Gill is then followed to a marshy col between Holmes Moss and Swarth Fell. The steep grassy flanks of Swarth Fell are then scaled before continuing on the classic ridge route to Wild Boar Fell.

From the summit a westerly descent is made passing Sand Tarn thence tracing its outflow, Clouds Gill past the outcrops of Fell End Clouds. An old track then descends to The Street, a minor road which leads back to Rawthey Bridge.

GREAT SHUNNER FELL - a circular from Thwaite

Distance 8 miles - moderate to strenuous

This popular Pennine Way route begins by following the Keld road out of Thwaite. At ref. 889983 the road is left for a walled track which climbs westwards over high pastures to the north of Thwaite Beck. An obvious cairned path then climbs the open moorland circumventing the head of the valley to reach the spacious top of the fell.

The descent can be varied by heading eastwards across peaty moors to Little Shunner Fell and thence south eastwards to the Buttertubs Pass keeping the summit of Lovely Seat directly ahead. The delightful road which offers beautiful vistas of Swaledale, is then used to return to Thwaite.

The Cam High Road, Wether Fell – a Roman highway

Looking across Cautley Crags to Yarlside (route 6)

THE HOWGILL FELLS

THE CALF

Route 6 - Circular from Cautley

YARLSIDE & KENSGRIFF

Route 7 - Circular from Handley's Bridge

FELL HEAD

Route 8 - Circular from Carlin Gill

ADDITIONAL INFORMATION

O.S. Landranger 1:50000 maps No.98 'Wensleydale & Upper Wharfedale' and (for Carlingill route) No 97 'Kendal to Morecambe'; O.S.Pathfinder Map 1:25000 sheet 607 for the Howgills; Harvey Map 1:40000 The Howgills

ACCOMMODATION

Cross Keys (temperance) at Cautley nr Sedbergh (A683); Cross Keys, Tebay (05874.240); Mrs E. Mattinson, Ash Hining Farm, Howgill (05396.20957); Dalesman Country Inn, Sedbergh (05396.21183).
Youth Hostel at Tebay
3 camp-sites at Sedbergh and 1 at Ravonstondale.

Railway Stations at Garsdale (on the Leeds - Carlisle Line) also Kendal (for Sedbergh).

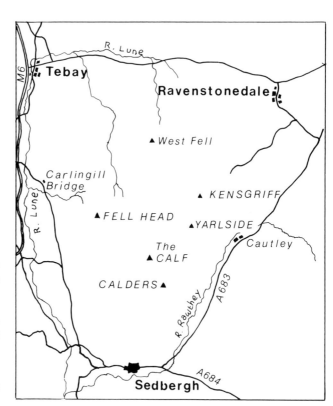

Climbing Hare Shaw above Cautley Spout towards The Calf

THE HOWGILL FELLS

The Howgill Fells are steep-sided grassy fells more akin to Lakeland than the Pennines for they consist of slates and shales rather than limestone. Strangely bereft of walls or fences, they are ideal for unrestricted high rambles. One look at the map reveals a very complex system of hills and valleys with few rocks or buttresses except the magnificent Cautley Crag or those that hem in Carlin Gill in its upper reaches.

Highest of the Howgills is the Calf at 2220 feet closely followed by Calders, Bram Rigg Top, Great Dummacks, Fell Head and Yarlside. Long lonely valleys cut deep into fellsides from the north, namely Bowderdale, Langdale and Weasdale. These make excellent approaches for long summers' day treks - or maybe for backpackers seeking a remote mountain campsite (The sunset over Morecambe Bay and the Lakeland fells is exquisite!).

When Wainwright first wrote his marvellous guide book he emphasised the solitude experienced on the Howgills. Although routes from Sedbergh and Cautley are now well used much of the region still possesses this intrinsic quality.

Route 6
THE CALF - A circular from Cautley

Distance 5 miles - short but steep & fairly strenuous

This spectacular walk begins from the Cross Keys Hotel (ref.698968) on the A683 road between Sedbergh and Kirkby Stephen. There are roadside spaces for the car but arrive early or you will have to use the Handley's Bridge lay-by a mile to the north.

A great deal of excitement is generated from the opening scene. Beyond the rushing River Rawthey, which flows parallel to the road, the meadows quickly soar to the typically steep Howgill flanks. The grassy theme is broken by the dark cliffs and screes of Cautley Crag. They span for nearly a mile between Great Dummacks and Yarlside's southern slopes. At their northern edge Cautley Spout, an impressive waterfall plummets in a series of foaming cascades confined by a narrow tree-lined ravine.

The route begins by a signpost marked 'to Cautley Spout' and we enter into this magnificent hillscape by crossing the footbridge over the Rawthey. The path turns left before reaching the valley of Cautley Holme Beck. It now climbs upstream in a grassy arena flanked by steep hillslopes with the crags and cascades directly ahead. As the valley narrows, the path divides. The one to the left goes directly to the falls - it is probably worth a detour if time allows but the climb from the waterfalls to the felltops is too steep to be recommended. Our route therefore takes the right fork on a path which skirts the scree slopes on Yarlside's flanks. This route gives lofty views of both crags and falls.

As the path reaches Bowderdale Head between Yarlside and the Calf it is abandoned. A left turn is made here to climb the steep trackless slopes of Hare Shaw. After crossing a slight hollow a prominent track, which has climbed out of

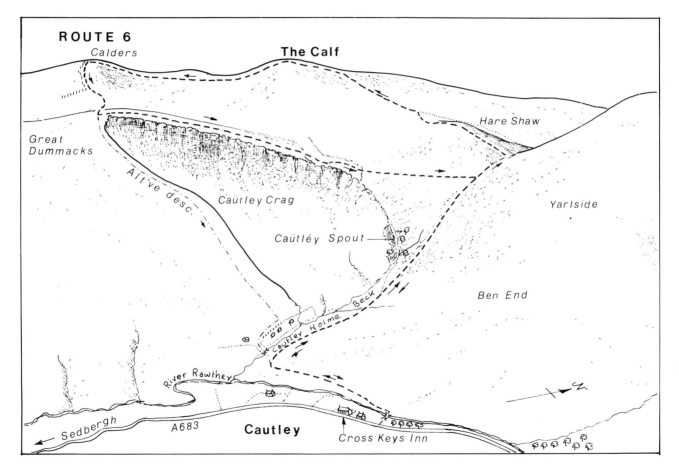

ROUTE 6

Calders

The Calf

Hare Shaw

Great Dummacks

Alt've desc.

Cautley Crag

Yarlside

Cautley Spout

Ben End

Cautley Holme Beck

River Rawthey

Sedbergh

A683

Cautley

Cross Keys Inn

Cautley Crags as seen from the Kirkby Stephen road

Bowderdale, is used for the final assault on The Calf.

The views from the Calf's trig point are magnificent, especially those of the Lake District, where many of the favoured peaks can be seen over the great ridge of High Street. Looking south-east, Pen-y-Ghent and Whernside are prominent. Ingleborough is largely obscured by Calders but its flat top just peeps out from behind the summit. The way forward is in that direction. The firm terrain allows easy walking on a broad track which straddles the undulating ridge. After passing the shoulder of the minor peak of Bram Rigg Top it reaches Calders, the Howgill's number two fell. From the large cairn on Calders a fence guides the way eastwards towards Great Dummacks. In a depression between the two fells the fence turns westwards and is of no further use to navigation. A continuation along the same bearing will however lead to the top.

The view from Great Dummacks along Cautley Crags to Yarlside is spectacular for the awesome scale of the cliffs and screes can truly be appreciated from this vantage. There are two alternative descents available from here. The first follows an obvious path tracing the edge of the crags before turning left by some prominent rocks to cross Red Gill Beck (not named on 1:50000 maps). It continues northwards to cross another beck (679975) above Cautley Spout. A well defined but narrow path now continues northwards to meet the Bowderdale Head path used on the outward journey. Steps are then retraced back to the Cross Keys Inn.

An alternative route from Great Dummacks would be to descend its north-eastern slopes, keeping to the east of the crags. Due to the steepness of these slopes, the route is

definitely not recommended in wintry conditions. At the bottom, Cautley Holme Beck is crossed via a small footbridge by an old barn. The route of ascent is then met and retraced to the Cross Keys Hotel where non-alcoholic refreshments such as coffee and cake are available at peak times.

Route 7
YARLSIDE - A circular from Handley's Bridge via Wandale and Kensgriff

Distance 7¹/₂ miles - fairly strenuous on steep slopes

This fine circular walk entails a gradual ascent above the serene valley of Wandale before crossing open moorland to climb the summits of Kensgriff and Yarlside. The latter, at 2097 ft. (639 metres) is one of the Howgill's highest peaks and, on a clear day, offers rewarding views. The walk should not be attempted in icy conditions as steep exposed slopes are encountered near the tops.

The walk begins at Handley's Bridge (ref.706977) five miles north-east of Sedbergh along the A683 Kirkby Stephen Road. A nearby lay-by provides convenient car-parking. The bridge is used to cross the River Rawthey, which flows swiftly through a patchwork of fields and hedgerows. A left turn along a cart track is made at the far side of the bridge. The steep slopes of Great Dummacks, which lie ahead, dominate the scene and kindle an anticipation for the high fell tops that are encountered in the latter stages of the walk. For the moment the terrain that lies ahead is one of a gentle nature. At

Walking south from Arant Haw in the Howgill Fells

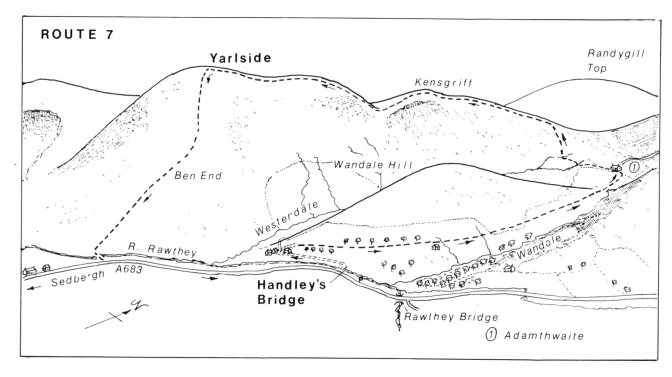

ROUTE 7

Yarlside

Randygill Top

Kensgriff

Ben End

Wandale Hill

Westerdale

Wandale

R. Rawthey

A683

Sedbergh

Handley's Bridge

Rawthey Bridge

① Adamthwaite

Narthwaite the track doubles back to traverse Wandale Hill's eastern slopes along a grassy terrace lined with gnarled hawthorns. After half a mile the entrancing ruins of Wandale are reached. The old farm is set in an attractive position amongst a glade of trees - a place to linger and survey the charming Wandale Valley and the dominating whaleback form of Harter Fell which lies to the north east.

The old track continues down the length of Wandale to reach the remote hill farm of Adamthwaite at its head. From here it turns westwards to climb through reedy pastures and thence follow the course of a dry-stone wall to the left. As the brow of the moor is crossed, new views unfold. The grand high ridge of Randy Gill Top sprawls across the western skyline and the conically shaped Kensgriff, our first summit, appears to the left of the scene. The wall is crossed via a stile and Adamthwaite Sike (stream) is forded. The route, sketchy underfoot, now follows the southern banks of the sike avoiding the more distinct path which turns south descending into Westerdale (the valley of Backside Beck). The rough, open moorland at the head of Westerdale is contoured crossing Spen Gill (a feeder stream to Backside Beck) above the gorge and then Stockless Gill where a steep sided ravine must be negotiated above the waterfalls.

A direct assault on Kensgriff's north eastern flanks is now made. The impressive vee shaped valley of Great Randy Gill is sighted to the west en route to the summit. Kensgriff is an amiable peak but is somewhat upstaged by its loftier neighbours. Most prominent is Yarlside, whose broad mass captivates one's attention and promises greater views.

A short, steep descent is made southwards to the saddle followed by an even sharper ascent of Yarlside's eastern escarpment to attain the summit ridge. This is followed in a south-westerly direction to reach the top, marked by a modest pile of stones. Here the real prize of the walk is claimed. A stunning western panorama of the Howgill's high, rolling crests, supplemented in clear conditions by the more distant craggy outlines of the splendid Lakeland Peaks. Such a spectacle is hard to leave behind but the descent along the south west flank to Ben End reveals another marvellous view of the range's most awesome feature - the harsh cliffs and scree slopes of Cautley and the tumbling cascades of its spout. The unrelentingly steep descent is completed by the banks of the River Rawthey, crossed via the footbridge north west of the Cross Keys Inn (no ale is served here, just coffee!). The A 683 Kirkby Stephen road is then followed northwards for 2/3 mile back to the start by Handley's bridge.

Route 8
FELL HEAD - A circular from Carlingill Bridge

Distance 5 miles - A rough scramble by Black Force followed by steep ascent to summit. This walk becomes difficult when the streams are in spate or in wintry conditions.

The Howgill's western approaches are generally less popular than those from Sedbergh or Cautley. This one is a short but exhilarating exploration of one of the Dales' most spectacular corners and begins from the old Roman Road between Sedbergh and Tebay at ref. 624995. Road-side parking spaces for cars are available fifty yards to the south at Gibbet Hill. The northern banks of Carlingill Beck are traced before crossing its first tributary (un-mamed). From here a narrow path climbs the lower grassy flanks of Uldale Head before traversing its southern slopes parallel to the beck. The lofty position of this track offers better views of the surrounding fells than the more used lower route. As the valley becomes more enclosed and bends to the left, a craggy cleft comes into view.

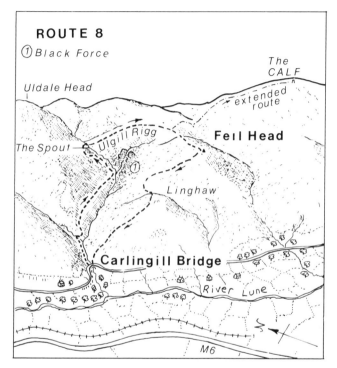

ROUTE 8

① *Black Force*

Uldale Head

The CALF

extended route

Feil Head

The Spout — Ulgill Rigg

①

Linghaw

Carlingill Bridge

River Lune

M6

Black Force

The path descends to the now rough and rocky riverbed and the scene is transformed. The rocky declivity seen earlier now reveals a superb waterfall - Black Spout. Foaming cascades plummet from a vee shaped nick in dark, strangely striated crags, to the mother stream a couple of hundred feet below. A path climbs steeply on a craggy spur to the left, but it is better to continue along the rough banks of Carlingill Beck to view another waterfall. The Spout, as it is known, is a thirty foot cascade hemmed in by steep slopes of friable shale. To the left is a diagonally ribbed crag which can be scaled to reach the top of the falls. The beck is now forded and a real slog begins on the steep grassy spur of Ulgill Rigg to reach the ridge east of Fell Head. The walk is easy from now on and the views westwards tremendous. They are at their best when Fell Head itself is attained. This is done by following the narrow, but well-used path south westwards. The summit is marked by a pile of stones and overlooks the fertile farmlands of the Lune Valley and out to sea over Morecambe Bay. Prominent are Killington Lake and the Lakeland Peaks. To the north is Cross Fell. The strange dome-like construction on the ridge is part of a radar and weather station on Great Dun Fell.

On the homeward journey a north westerly descent is made at the head of Fairmile Beck. It reveals intimate views of the Lune Gorge, once one of England's finest valleys. The rural charm and natural lines of the landscape have now been unceremoniously and unashamedly severed by the unsightly M6 motorway. By comparison the railway, part of the Euston to Glasgow line, seems sympathetic to its surroundings.

The path declines to a col, east of Linghaw. After scaling the little peak it descends north westwards, returning to Carlingill Bridge.

FELL HEAD to The CALF

The walk can be extended to climb to the Calf by following the prominent ridge path from Fell Head ENE to Breaks Head (ref. 654985 -not named on 1:50000 maps). A south easterly

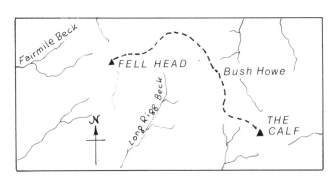

descent is then made to a col before climbing to Bush Howe and thence to the Calf. From here the possible routes are endless although all rather long. Probably the best option would be to descend White Fell with a stream crossing at the confluence of Long Rigg and Calf Becks before using a farm track past Castley to reach the old Roman Road three miles south of Carlingill Bridge.

THE HOWGILL SPINE - Bowderdale to Sedbergh
Distance 12 miles - moderate to hard

This long walk bites deep into the lonely heart of Howgills. It begins at Bowderdale Foot (ref. 676047) on a cul-de-sac south of the busy A685 road. After following a cart track southwards to open fell a vehicle track is followed to climb (half right) out of the valley to West Fell then southwards along the ridge to Hazelgill Knott. It continues to the Calf's summit. A fine promenade then follows over Bram Rigg Top and Calders and Arant Haw before descending steeply to the east of Winder to Lockbank Farm on the northern outskirts of Sedbergh.

On The Calf's summit looking west to the Lakeland Hills

THE EASTERN PEAKS

GREAT WHERNSIDE

Route 9 A Circular form Kettlewell

BUCKDEN PIKE

Route 10 A Circular from Kettlewell

Route 11 From Starbotton

CRACOE FELL

Route 12 A Circular from Rylstone

ADDITIONAL INFORMATION

Maps for Gt Whernside & Buckden Pike - O.S. Landranger 1:50000 No. 98 'Wensleydale & Upper Wharfedale';   1:25000 Leisure Map Yorkshire Dales Northern &   Central Areas. For Cracoe Fell - O.S. Landranger 1:50000 No 103 'Blackburn & Burnley'; Outdoor Leisure No 10 'Yorkshire Dales Southern Area'

ACCOMMODATION

The Racehorses (075676.233) The Bluebell (075676.230) and the Kings Head (075676.242) plus many guest houses at Kettlewell. THe Buck Inn at Buckden (075676.227); Tennant Arms, Kilnsey. (0756.752301)
Youth Hostels at Kettlewell, Linton (Grassington) and Aysgarth
Camp-sites: Kettlewell; Wood Nook nr. Threshfield and Hawkswick Cote nr. Arncliffe.

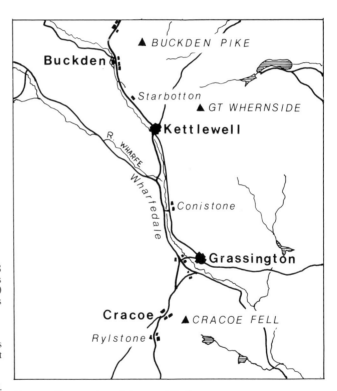

Nearest railway station - Skipton and Darlington.

GREAT WHERNSIDE

Anybody who has wondered why Great Whernside was so named when it has an inferior altitude to Ribblesdale's more famous Whernside will have their curiosity satisfied on the first visit to Wharfedale. From here it assumes true mountain proportions, soaring from the back yards of Kettlewell to the skyline. They will also be enthralled by the expansive panoramas seen from its airy, crag-strewn summit. On a clear day both coasts of England are just visible as are the Lakeland Mountains and most of the high Dales peaks.

Great Whernside's fine limestone topography above Wharfedale is topped by a thinly vegetated peaty ridge which declines in a complex system of ridges and spurs to the north and east.

Route 9
GREAT WHERNSIDE from Kettlewell

Distance 9 miles - fairly strenuous

Kettlewell is, in my opinion, the loveliest Dales' village. It has a mixture of stone and whitewashed dwellings huddled around the River Wharfe which meanders lazily amongst green fields. Broad leafed trees and dry-stone walls accentuate the graceful sweep of the lower hillslopes. Above them, the horizontal

Hag Dyke on the slopes of Gt. Whernside

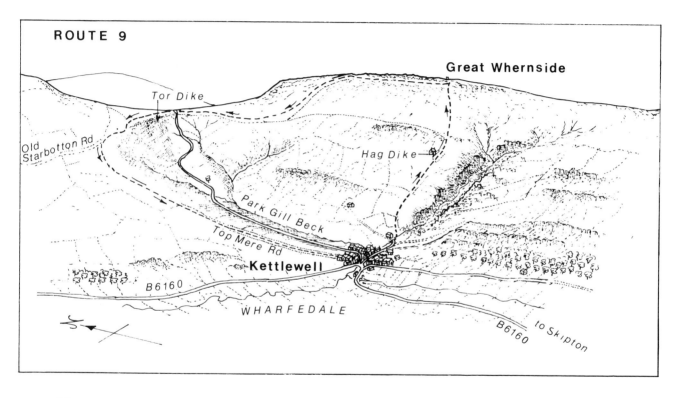

ROUTE 9

Great Whernside

Tor Dike

Old Starbotton Rd

Hag Dike

Park Gill Beck

Top Mere Rd

Kettlewell

B 6160

W H A R F E D A L E

B6160 to Skipton

strata of the pallid limestone terraces fringe the high slopes and add relief to this emerald scene. At the centre of Kettlewell is the tiny old bridge which spans Dowber Gill Beck. Two old white-washed coach-houses, the Bluebell Inn and Racehorses Hotel, lie adjacent to the bridge and face each other across the street. Around them are scores of charming stone-built cottages.

The road which traces the southern banks of Dowber Gill Beck is used to leave the village eastwards to Great

Whernside. It passes some beautifully renovated cottages with colourful riverbank gardens and terminates at an old chapel. A track then continues and crosses the beck by a camp-site. Two paths from here are clearly signposted and both are useable to the summit of Great Whernside. One strikes uphill for Hag Dike Farm, now a scout centre, and the other follows the beautiful course of Dowber Gill. The former is probably superior for the Dowber Gill route has an arduous climax on the marshy trackless slopes of Whernside Pasture.

The path to Hag Dyke is a simple one to follow on a firm grassy spur. It affords views into Dowber Gill's limestone ravine and also retrospective views to Kettlewell and Old Cote Moor, which are increasingly breathtaking as height is gained. At Hag Dyke Farm, the terrain changes from high pasture to moorland, and a steep course on stony slopes ensues before the final pull over peaty terrain.

Great Whernside's summit is a grand one, capped with dark gritstone crags and boulders. Its concrete trig point is dwarfed by a large cairn set proud of the huge boulders. In southern panoramas Wharfedale can be traced until the lower slopes above Conistone obscure its change of direction. The well known overhanging Kilnsey Crag is clearly discernible

The summit of Great Whernside looking across Wharfedale

as are the plains of Lancashire paling to the Irish Sea beyond. To the west, across Old Cote Moor, the distinctive profile of Pen-y-Ghent and the less shapely Fountains Fell lead the eye to the distant Lakeland Fells. In one of my more memorable fell-walks I decided to camp on the summit. It was fairly near mid-summer and the day had been a scorcher. After setting camp and eating some good hot curry I watched the sun set slowly over the western dales. In the last light the mountains on the horizon became clearer and stood out against the fiery skies and I could easily recognise my favourite summits.

The homeward route continues northwards along the ridge to the parish border fence close to the 667 meter spot height. A descent is then made on a good path which follows Tor Dyke. This earthwork was built by Iron Age Brigante chief, Venutius around AD70 in order to close off the valley heads and thus strengthen his defensive position against the Romans. This was only part of his organised network which included forts on Ingleborough and Addleborough. He was, however eventually defeated at Stanwick by the Ninth Legion who had marched from York, led by Petilius Cerialis.

A high and lonely lane linking Wharfedale and Coverdale bisects the dyke. It is crossed and the path continues westwards following the old earthwork rounding the ravine formed by Fears Gill Beck to reach the Starbotton Road (track). This leads south westwards to a signposted junction of ancient roads at Cam Head. The descent is made on the Top Mere Road which gives delightful views down lovely Wharfedale. The easy paced decline makes a fitting finale to a grand mountain walk. Kettlewell's cafés and inns now await you for well deserved refreshment.

BUCKDEN PIKE

Like Great Whernside, Buckden Pike parades its finest face to Wharfedale. Tiered, tree-clad slopes dwarf the tiny villages of Cray, Buckden and Starbotton. The uniformity of these western slopes is broken by the crag-rimmed combes formed by Cam Gill and Buckden Becks.

The one mile long summit plateau is grassy and usually very firm although the approaches to it are rather more squelchy. To the north east of the summit, the mountain is dissected by the lonely, vee-shaped Walden Valley. The two resuling peat-hagged ridges resembe a lobster's claw when seen on the map. The northern ridge descends to Bishopdale whilst the longer southern arm ends abruptly at Penhill whose precipitous slopes plummet into Wensleydale.

Tor Mere Top, the southernmost extremity of Buckden Pike's summit ridge, overlooks the huge verdant hollow of Park Gill. To the west of the gill, a grassy spur declines via Cam Head to Kettlewell. On the opposite flank is Great Whernside. A narrow winding lane from Kettlewell climbs out of the hollow to a high pass which links Great Whernside with Buckden Pike and separates Park Gill and Coverdale.

Although inferior in height to Great Whernside, Buckden Pike is probably more popular. This is in part due to the profusion of superb ancient tracks and roads which entice walkers to climb to its wild windswept and typically Pennine summit plateau. This is one of Yorkshire's most pleasant places with wide, inspiring views over several counties.

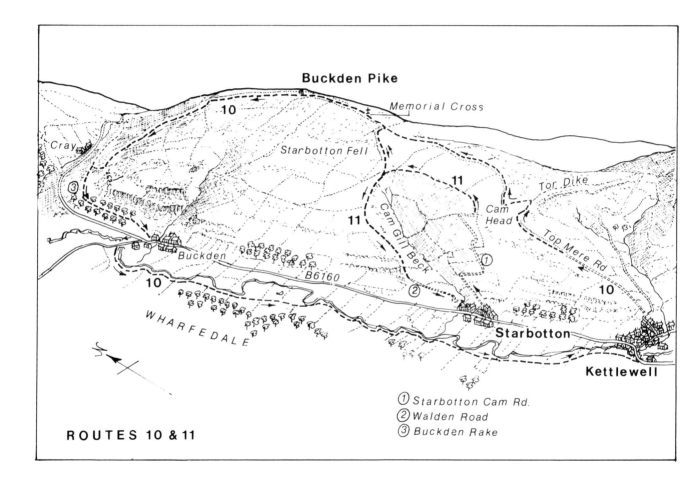

Buckden Pike

Memorial Cross

Cray

Starbotton Fell

10

11

11

Cam Gill Beck

Cam Head

Tor Dike

Top Mere Rd

③

Buckden

B6160

10

① **10**

②

WHARFEDALE

Starbotton

Kettlewell

① *Starbotton Cam Rd.*
② *Walden Road*
③ *Buckden Rake*

R O U T E S 10 & 11

Route 10
BUCKDEN PIKE - A Circular from Kettlewell

Distance 13 miles - strenuous

Kettlewell provides the longest and probably most satisfying ascent of Buckden Pike and there's ample space for car parking. The Coverdale road, signposted 'to Leyburn', is followed to a sharp bend (ref. 972725) where we switch to a walled track known as the Top Mere Road. This climbs steadily over a high grassy spur separating the valleys of Wharfedale and Park Gill. Looking back, Kettlewell sits snugly, surrounded by a patchwork of fields which gently contour the tree studded hillslopes. The valley is enclosed by the terraced limestone crags of Old Cote Moor to the west and the majestic soaring slopes of Great Whernside in the east. Mike Harding in his book "Walking the Dales" considers this to be one of the classic views of Yorkshire. At Cam Head the track meets the Starbotton road. A left turn along this open 'green road' leads to the walled Starbotton Cam Road. Just beyond the first gate ((965754) it is abandoned for a track which climbs NNE before in turn being abandoned at the next dry-stone wall (966755). A grooved path then climbs eastwards to gain the ridge. The route now continues northwards following the line of the ridge wall to Tor Mere Top.

    The route northwards from Tor Mere Top can be a bit marshy. In mist the deviations of the ridge wall can be confusing especially on the path's junction with the old Walden Road. It would be very easy to be drawn along this

On the summit of Buckden Pike

prominent track down into the Walden Valley.

    Sited on the southern end of Buckden Pike's summit massif is a solitary cross and plaque - a memorial to the Polish crew of a World War II plane which crashed into the fell during a violent snow storm. There was one survivor. He had sustained a broken leg, but crawled out of the wreckage to find some fox tracks. On deducing that in such harsh weather the fox would be looking for easy pickings close to human civilization, he followed the footprints. Indeed these did lead to a farmhouse.

In thanksgiving for his own life and in memorial for his five colleagues, he had the memorial cross built. Embedded in the concrete are pieces of wreckage from the plane and also a brass foxes head.

Leaving the Memorial Cross, the wall is followed to Buckden Pike's summit which is crowned by a cairn and trig point. Views have now widened and many of the Dales' notable summits can now be seen. Dominant in the south east across the sombre and extensive peatlands is Great Whernside. Most eyes will be transfixed by the western horizon where Fountains Fell, Pen-y-Ghent, Ingleborough and Whernside vie for supremacy. Further north are the more distant fells of Wild Boar and Great Shunner. If the atmospheric conditions are good you will see the angular profiles of Lakeland Hills on the far western horizon.

The initial descent from Buckden Pike is guided by a dry-stone wall down steep western flanks. Signposts and a line of wooden stakes make the well used path easy to follow as it changes direction, gradually veering to the south west. On further descent, the village of Cray appears, tucked close to the sides of Cow Pasture. Walls radiate from the village fields to the high moors rather like a section from a huge spider's web. In the valley below, Cray Gill tumbles in a series of picturesque waterfalls to meet the River Wharfe which meanders in low plains beneath wooded lower hillslopes.

The mountain path meets a well used ancient road known as Buckden Rake at ref.941785. A left turn is made along the track which descends into Wharfedale entering Rakes Wood before reaching the delightful village of Buckden. The best course for a return to Kettlewell is part of the delightful 'Dales Way'. To reach it take the Hubberholme Road out of the village (Dubbs Lane) and leave it beyond the bridge over the River Wharfe. The well signposted route closely follows the western banks for most of the four miles back to Kettlewell.

Route 11
BUCKDEN PIKE from Starbotton

Distance 7¹/₂ miles (round trip) - moderate

Starbotton's stone-built cottages huddle in the shelter of Buckden Pike's western slopes close to the ravine of Cam Gill. The village was once home to the many lead-miners who toiled on the lofty surrounding hillsides. The charming white-washed Fox and Hounds Inn, built in Georgian times, is the centre-piece of the community. In 1686 the quietude of the scene was horrendously disrupted when freak storms turned Cam Beck into a raging torrent. The water rose to tremendous heights and the resulting floods brought about the collapse of many cottages. Others were filled with mud and debris ripped from the mountainsides.

The route starts from the village centre on a cul-de-sac to the south of the inn. At its eastern extremity is a stony walled track known as the Starbotton Cam Road. This immediately tackles the hillslopes, zig-zagging above hawthorn clad pastures fringed with limestone crag. To the north the playful Cam Gill Beck is seen in the shade of the curiously named Knuckle Bone Pasture which soars to the peaty top of Starbotton

Fell. The road is left at ref.965753, a few yards before the gate which marks its entry onto the open fellsides. Here an ancient green track climbs NNE then northwards across airy slopes high above Cam Gill. Eastern views are obscured by Tor Mere Top but to the west Wharfedale is laid beneath your feet. Pen-y-Ghent has peaked its head above the flanks of Old Cote Moor and Whernside can be seen on the northern horizon over the shoulder of Yockenthwaite Moor. After passing the spoil heaps of old lead mines, the path joins the old Walden Road at the head of Cam Gill (ref. 962772) and the route follows this road north eastwards over Starbotton Fell.

On attaining the ridge there are attractive views down to the Walden Valley. Beyond a gate (ref. 965776) the Walden Road is left for a path which climbs north westwards (left) over brown, peaty moors towards the summit plateau. The terrain can be quite marshy at times for the grass cover has been badly eroded. We are now on the route previously described (from Kettlewell) and pass the memorial cross en route to the summit.

It is possible to make a circular of this route by descending south westwards across rough pastures to the old Buckden Lead Mines (ref. 955782). Here a faint path declines to Starbotton. The path has fallen into disuse however and route finding is complex. A better way is to retrace steps back to the head of Cam Gill (ref.962772). This time continue along the Walden Road which descends Knuckle Bone Pasture to the west of Cam Gill. Views of Wharfedale are restricted but this descent reveals some waterfalls and is enhanced in the final stages by intimate views of Starbotton.

The Memorial Cross, Buckden Pike commemorating the deaths of five Polish Airmen during World War 2

CRACOE FELL

A wild tract of high heathery moorland sprawls from the Wharfedale villages of Bolton Abbey and Appletreewick to its summits at Thorpe Fell and Cracoe Fell, both just over 500 metres high. To the north and west the fells display a more exciting face. Fringed by dark gritstone cliffs and crags, their flanks plummet a thousand feet to the farm pastures of Thorpe, Cracoe and Rylstone. Beneath the northern edges are several small, rounded hills known as the Cracoe Reef Knolls. These curious mounds are rich in limestone fossils and now form part of a Site of Special Scientific Interest.

Although only one bridleway is shown on the maps the tops are covered by an access agreement. As long as you leave the dog at home you can wander at will.

Route 12
CRACOE FELL - A Circular from Rylstone

Distance 6 miles - fairly easy

This walk offers a short exploration of a rough, gritty fell set amongst an area of gentle rolling countryside at the edge of the Yorkshire Dales. There are a few car parking spots by the pond just off the main road at Rylstone Village. A short walk southwards along the busy Skipton Road brings us to a walled track, (972583). This is followed for half a mile before continuing eastwards on a signposted bridleway heading towards the craggy precipices of Rylstone Fell. Initially the route is sketchy. Keep to the right of a small plantation of Scots Pine ignoring the stony track which goes to their left. Above the plantation the right of way traverses an area of grass and reeds before meeting the track just short of a five-bar gate in a dry-stone wall.

The terrain becomes more peaty and heather clad as the track winds beneath crags in a deep groove. To the right the crusty ravine of Waterfall Gill and Embsay Moor add a sombre wildness to the landscape. This will be perpetuated for the rest of the walk. Just short of the next wall a grassy rutted track diverges from the main track. It narrows and veers left rounding a large gritstone outcrop to meet the main ridge wall. Although most travellers have kept to the east (right) of the wall I think it is better to stay on the left. This way intimate views of the dark precipices are maintained. The feeling on the other side is one of being imprisoned by this tall rampart which obscures the more interesting western prospects.

The first minor summit is adorned with a memorial cross set on a gigantic crag. The cross commemorates the Paris Treaty of 1813 following the Battle of Waterloo. Wide views to the west include the shapely peaks of Flasby Fell, the hills of Malham and, to the north, Buckden Pike. To the east is undulating moorland carpeted with heather and studded randomly with dark crags and boulders.

The way continues along the craggy edge, probably to the accompaniment of ravens, the odd grouse, pheasant or bird of prey. Half a mile north east of the cross the path becomes briefly tricky. The wall becomes rather close to the edge and large crags bar the way. The crags can either be climbed or

Buckden Pike and Wharfedale from above Kettlew

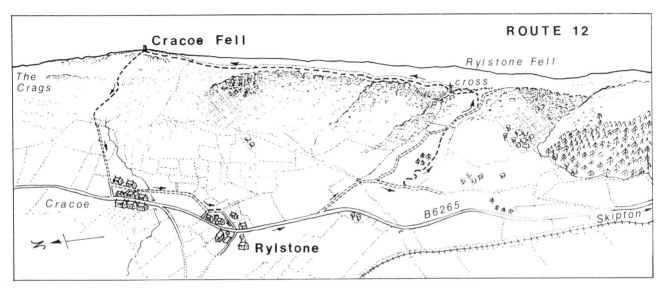

ROUTE 12

Cracoe Fell

Rylstone Fell

The Crags

cross

Cracoe

B6265

Skipton

Rylstone

circumvented. You do not need to go down too far.

After scaling a ladder stile at an intersection of walls the path climbs to the highest land at Watt Crag on the summit of Cracoe Fell. Perched on this huge boulder is an obelisk erected to remember the dead of the First World War. Views northwards have improved and the swelling ridge of Great Whernside can now be seen in its entirety.

There are no paths evident underfoot descending direct from Cracoe Fell. This can be considered confusing to some but I like to think that the slopes are free from erosion and the walker is free to roam. Pick your own course. The grassy western flanks are steep in places but not difficult or dangerous. We are aiming for the Fell Lane Track from Cracoe Village to ref. 987598. This lies to the left of a grassy Knoll (Skelterton Hill) and close to where the stream meets the intake wall. After descending the steep grassy slopes, an area of rough grassland and reeds is traversed to reach some sheep pens by the intake wall. A gate to the left of these gives access to a walled track which then leads to the village.

The track becomes metalled by a small cottage. A left turn is made on a back lane prior to the junction with the main road. This passes some pleasant cottages and the back of the

tarbotton from the Walden Road

Cracoe Fell from the old fishponds at Rylstone

Devonshire Arms before meeting another walled track, signposted 'Bridleway to Rylstone' This pleasant stony lane is followed parallel to the main road. It skirts a strange area of embankments marked as fish ponds on the map. This was formerly the village green. Beyond the fish ponds and farmhouse a narrow tarmac lane passes behind the square-towered nineteenth century parish church. Close to the church on the left hand side of the lane there are remnants of the Old Manor

House. This was once home to the Norton family whose fate was described in Wordsworth's 'The White Doe of Rylstone'. Some members of the family were executed for taking part in the Pilgrimage of Grace and the Rising of the North in 1569. Kit Norton also tried unsuccessfully to rescue Mary Queen of Scots from Bolton Castle in Wensleydale.

The lane finally meets the main road opposite to the pond in Rylstone's village centre where the journey is completed.

OTHER RECOMMENDED ROUTES

GREAT WHERNSIDE from Conistone

Distance 8¹/₂ miles (one way) 16 miles using circular via Kettlewell - strenuous

A hundred yards to the north of the village a track climbs eastwards past a TV mast through an extensive area of limestone crag. The track is abandoned as it crosses Mossdale Beck beneath Mossdale Scar(016697). A bridleway then traverses rough moorland to reach the ridge. The way to Great Whernside looks simple on the map but the ground underfoot is trackless and rough - full of peat haggs and thick heather. A ridge fence, however makes navigation in mist foolproof. For a return journey try descending to Kettlewell as described via Hag Dyke and thence follow the Dales Way (now marked on all O.S. Maps). This crosses low pastures around Kettlewell before climbing to lofty valleysides amongst the limestone cliffs. It meets the outward route close to the TV mast.

GREAT WHERNSIDE from Nidderdale

Distance 6¹/₂ miles (one way) - strenuous

Starts from the Scar House Reservoir car park (ref.068767). After crossing the reservoir, an ancient track, the Carle Fell Road is used to climb westwards up the barren slopes beneath Little Whernside to reach the ridge two miles north of the main summit.

BUCKDEN PIKE from Walden Head

Distance 2¹/₂ miles (one way)

The lonely Walden Valley has a narrow lane which terminates at Kentucky House. From here the old Walden Road will lead to the high fellsides. It begins a stony track terminating at some outbuildings at Walden Head a short way south. A signposted path is then followed down the valley on the western banks of Walden Beck (n.b. current maps show the track as being on the opposite banks). The stream, now Deepdale Beck, is forded close to its confluence with Fosse Beck before a signposted path climbs steeply up Walden Moor. On reaching the ridge, the old road is abandoned at a gate by a wall corner (ref. 965776). A sharp right turn then leads to the memorial cross and then to the main summit. The return journey can be shortened by descending westwards (trackless) picking up the Walden road at Groove End.

Ingleborough from Souther Scales

THE THREE PEAKS

INGLEBOROUGH

Route 13 Circular from Newby Cote
Route 14 From Ingleton
Route 15 From Chapel-le Dale
Route 16 A Circular from Austwick

WHERNSIDE

Route 17 Circular from Dent
Route 18 Circular From Ribblehead
Route 19 From Twisleton

PEN-Y-GHENT

Route 20 Circular from Horton
Route 21 From Foxup
Route 22 From Dale Head

ADDITIONAL INFORMATION

Outdoor Leisure Map 1:25000 No.2 'Western Area'; Landranger 1:50000 No 98 'Wensleydale and Upper Wharfedale'.

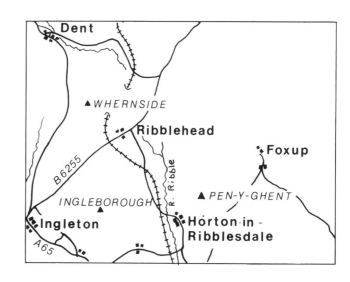

ACCOMMODATION;
The Crown, Horton-in-Ribblesdale (07296.209); Pen-y-Ghent Cafe, Horton (07296.333); Mrs. Pilkington, Middle Studfold Farm, Horton (07296.236); The New Inn, Clapham (04685.203);The Game Cock Inn, Austwick (04685.226); The Pines Country House Hotel, Ingleton (05242.41252). Youth Hostels at Ingleton and Stainforth;
Camp-sites at Holme Farm, Horton-in-Ribblesdale; Stainforth; Ingleton and Clapham (near railway station).

Railway Station; Horton-in Ribblesdale (Leeds - Carlisle) & Clapham. (Leeds - Morecambe/Lancaster).

INGLEBOROUGH

The well loved and majestic massif of Ingleborough crowns a triangle of high ground between the River Doe, River Ribble and the busy A65 trunk road. At its feet lie several charming villages including Chapel-le-Dale, Horton, Austwick, Clapham and the buzzing tourist centre of Ingleton.

A hard weather resistant cap of millstone grit has given the mountain its distinctive flat top whilst the underlying shales have been eroded into steep flanks which plunge to the expansive plinth of carboniferous limestone. In impressive and dramatic facades to the north and west of the summit precipitous slopes have been scoured by glaciers to reveal screes and jutting terraces of dark severe crags. Below them is a shelf of rough grassland terminating at the limestone terraces of Raven and White Scars which, in turn, descend steeply in steps to the River Doe.

Little Ingleborough lies one mile to the south of the main peak and at the edge of an escarpment which rises boldly from the vast moorlands of Newby Moss. To the north of Ingleborough is the grassy eminence of Simon Fell. A narrow ridge connecting the two fells gives them an hour glass formation when viewed on the map. In one of the resulting combes known as Clapham Bents, Fell Beck surfaces before cascading three hundred feet into a the gargantuan pot hole of Gaping Gill. It reappears as Clapham Beck in a sylvan valley to the north of Clapham village.

Ingleborough is synonymous with its limestone scenery and some of the most spectacular features are seen around Moughton to the west of Horton-in-Ribblesdale. Here a wide area is covered by clints, pavements, dry valleys and pot holes. In addition to being a spectacular geological composition, Ingleborough is steeped in history. Borough means fortified place and indeed, close to its summit, there are traces of an ancient fort believed to have been constructed by the Brigantes

Ingleborough's summit

tribe who retreated to the mountain during Roman times. There are also remains of circular stone shelters dating back to the iron age.

The summit cairn was built on the ruins of a tower which was constructed in 1830 and subsequently wrecked by inebriated participants of the opening ceremony. Near to the trig. point is a cross-shaped stone shelter which has a view indicator built into its centre and what a view! The lakeland mountains, Snowdon in Wales, and the Isle of Man's Snaefell are all included in a vast panorama. When the weather smiles it is an opportunity for the seasoned walker to linger on the summit plateau when the impending darkness has sent others scurrying homeward. The reward can be great for the setting sun bathes the landscape with a pink light, highlighting pale

Newby Moss from Little Ingleborough

limestone scars and casting shadows in the wall-patterned pastures. The River Wenning glistens, meandering through the low plains and leading the eye to the Irish Sea, shimmering bright gold under a fiery sky.

The popularity of Ingleborough will inevitably mean that its magnificent mountainscapes will have to be shared with many other walkers but it is a small penalty for such scenic grandeur.

Route 13
INGLEBOROUGH from Newby Cote

Distance 10 miles - moderate to hard

On weekends and in the summer months Ingleborough's majestic appeal makes it a much frequented hill but this little used ascent from Newby Cote offers those who require a little solitude an interesting route to the summit.

Starting at map ref.732705 a northbound track is followed through the hamlet of Newby Cote. After passing over a stile the line of a wall on the left points the way to the open moor. As further height is gained the dour sights of the barren lower slopes are superseded by a more interesting landscape. First to catch the attention are the limestone scars of Clapdale which make a welcome overture to the first sighting of Pen-y-Ghent lying beyond in views to the east. To the west of the route, just north of Grey Scars, are the many pot-holes of Newby Moss (well worth a detour when time is of no

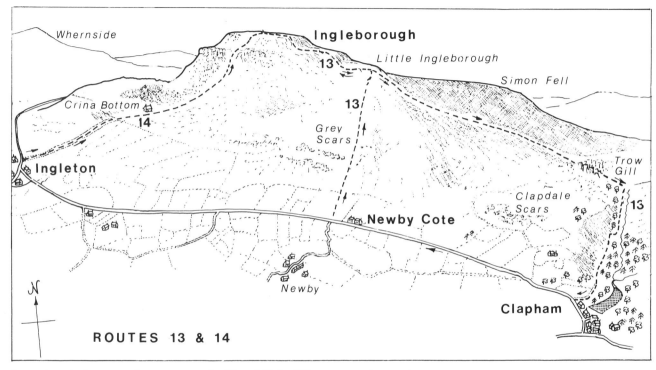

ROUTES 13 & 14

importance). Amongst the group are the Fluted Hole, Pillar Hole, and also Long Kin West Pot, which is a fearsome fissure some three-hundred feet deep.

For half the walk the monotonous concave lower slopes obscure the famous and noble profile of Ingleborough's summit mass but as the grassy shoulder of the moor is reached the toils are rewarded with a spectacle of mountain scenery unrivalled within the county of Yorkshire. Ingleborough finally appears. The dark towering gritstone crags which crown a broad limestone shelf above White Scars and Ingleborough

Common tantalize the walker who will be at this stage eagerly anticipating the final approaches.

Rather than aiming directly for the summit, however, the best line of approach is via Little Ingleborough, where a large cairn acts as an excellent marker for the route ahead. The bastions of millstone grit guarding the summit seem totally impregnable but a narrow path which cuts diagonally across the eastern face makes this a deceptively easy approach.

On descending, steps are first retraced Little Ingleborough. To the south, the moorland seen below is dappled with hundreds of sink holes resembling craters in a lunar landscape. A sketchy path descends south eastwards over the steep slopes of Little Ingleborough to reach Fell Beck which is followed southwards to Gaping Gill. Here its chattering waters tumble three hundred and forty feet into an enormous cavern which opens out below. Rickety perimeter fences serve as a warning that this is a very dangerous place and attempts at close inspection are not recommended. (Little can be seen for the strongest sunlight does not penetrate far below the surface of this dark chasm.)

The track continues southwards before veering to the south west to enter the a shallow valley which deepens and narrows into the gorge-like ravine of Trow Gill where the waters of Fell Beck would once have furiously flowed. Careful scrambling is required to negotiate the slippery boulders which mar the way through the dark confines of the gill's narrow kneck.

Beyond Trow Gill the path turns right (south) along a widening partially wooded limestone valley. Thwaite Scars are revealed high on the open hillsides to the east. The path then passes by the entrance to Ingleborough Cave, a wonderland of caverns and passages opened to the public by James and Oliver Farrer in 1837. Guided tours amongst the stalactites and stalagmites are frequently taken and timetables of these are displayed by the entrance. Close by is Beck Head where the waters of Fell Beck resurface and are now renamed Clapham Beck.

At ref.754707, opposite a footbridge over Clapham Beck, a path which climbs steeply to Clapdale Farm is followed. The austere dwelling surrounded by windswept pines was once the home of the witch of Clapham. From it, a track, the Clapdale Lane continues southwards. Its lofty position offers superb views over the valley where the woodland spread is increased and includes Silver Firs, sweet chestnut and scots pines. The lane declines close to the western shores of Clapham's fine lake - a scene decorated by rhododendrons which thrive in the sheltered valley and also by sitka spruce. The artificial lake was formed in the nineteenth century by damming Clapham Beck. It not only supplied water to the village but was also an integral part of a hydro-electric scheme which supplied power for street lighting in days when the facility was uncommon.

The route from the foot of Clapdale lane follows the old Ingleton Lane back to Newby Cote, a distance of one mile but a short detour into picturesque Clapham is highly recommended. The small village is situated in a niche sheltered by woodland and craggy hillsides. It remains offset and unperturbed by the busy A65 trunk road which by-passes to the south. Clapham Beck flows briskly under pleasing small single-arched bridges and close to the rustic stone-built cottages and square-towered church. There is also a café and pub for well earned refreshments before undertaking that last mile back to Newby Cote.

Route 14
INGLEBOROUGH from Ingleton

Distance 4 miles - moderate

This popular and direct route, which climbs the mountain from the south west, reveals exquisite views of its precipitous western facades. Its steep and rocky upper reaches can provide the experienced walker with exciting scrambling in wintery conditions.

The path begins at ref.702731 just to east of Ingleton village on the B6255 'Hawes' road and crosses Storrs Common to the south of Storrs Cave. The Fell Lane walled track, which is then utilised, climbs steadily, passing below the broken limestone terraces at the southern edge of White Scars. The lane terminates at Crina Bottom Farm where a cherished scene, which has graced many postcards, is suddenly revealed. In it the farmhouse nestles amongst a wooded glade bordering shapely limestone outcrops. These lead the eye to the towering mass of Ingleborough whose jutting white crags are thrown into sharp relief against the sky.

The path leaves the track to climb the wet grassy slopes of Red Gait Head to the north of Hard Gill. At the 490 metre contour a collection of three potholes lie to the north of the route and a detour could be made in order to see them. The most interesting is Quaking Pot, a dark circular void into which tumbles a thin spout-like waterfall.

The climb stiffens to go above the first tier of limestone crags, relents briefly before a final scramble over loose gritstone rocks amongst the upper gritstone tier. It is then no more than a short walk north-eastwards from the plateau's edge to the summit cairn.

A possible variation for the return to Ingleton would be to descend via the Newby Cote route and thence along the back road to Ingleton. This would make a ten mile round trip.

Route 15
INGLEBOROUGH from Chapel-le Dale

Distance: 2¹/₂ miles (one way) - short but stiff climb

This short route from the Old Hill Inn provides some of Ingleborough's finest prospects and visits the caves of Great Douk and Middle Washfold en route.

Cars can be parked for a small fee on the car park adjacent to the inn (ref.743777). The B6255 Ingleton to Hawes road is followed eastwards for a couple of hundred yards. Here a stile to the right is crossed and a broad track followed over pastureland passing between an old lime kiln and a perched boulder. From the onset the majestic lines of Ingleborough rivet one's attention. Assuming gargantuan proportions, its steep western flanks plummet in a graceful sweep from its flat

Approaching Ingleborough on the shoulder of Simon Fell

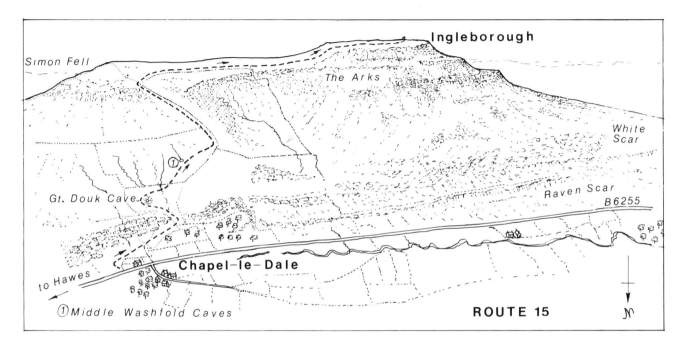

Ingleborough

Simon Fell

The Arks

White Scar

Raven Scar

B 6255

Gt. Douk Cave

① Middle Washfold Caves

to Hawes

Chapel–le–Dale

ROUTE 15

summit plateau to the broad limestone shelf some six hundred feet below.

After scaling two stiles over cross walls the path turns sharply to the east and a tree-filled crater is encountered. This is the site of Great Douk Cave. A stream pouring out of a great cleft in the limestone marks its position. An underground passage connects this cave to Middle Washfold but it is no place for the inexperienced - better to follow the surface route.

The Middle Washfold Caves, which lie just one third of a mile to the south close to the path, would better be described as fissures than caves. Underground passages can be entered here if the streams that flow in them are not in spate. From the caves the path continues southwards to a dry-stone wall. The nature of the walk now changes abruptly and there is only one way to go - up! The arduous climb on the steep north western flanks of Souther Scales Fell has no laudable attributes except to reveal the splendid view of Ribblehead viaduct. A study of the dry-stone wall accompanying the climb reveals that, like the mountain itself, there is a transition from limestone to gritstone as height is gained.

The climb finishes as abruptly as it began and, from the north western edge of Simon Fell, an easy flat path allows idyllic, carefree striding with the imposing Ingleborough massif filling the scene ahead. Its summit plateau is gained after a short easy scramble over broken gritstone crags.

Unfortunately the obvious return route descending the saddle between Ingleborough and Simon Fell is now closed due to horrible erosion. Possible alternatives would be to descend via the Ingleton route diverting from ref. 710734 past Skirwith Cave to the B6255 road which would then be followed north eastwards for 3 miles back to the start. Another route would retrace steps to Simon Fell then continue along the

Traversing Moughton Scars with Ingleborough on the skyline

ridge to Park Fell, the eastern outlier of the group. A NE descent to New Close would then meet a footpath (ref.772779) traversing an interesting area of pot-holes and outcrops westwards to the B road less than a mile east of the Old Hill Inn.

Route 16
INGLEBOROUGH - A Circular from Austwick via Moughton Scars & Trow Gill

---

Distance: 12 miles - strenuous

The fields of Crummackdale are hemmed in on three sides by a massive area of limestone cliffs, outcrops and pavements. The quiet village of Austwick, lying at the southern end of the dale, is an ideal base for a long exploration of Ingleborough.

From the village centre take the lane northwards passing Town Head Farm. The narrow, winding lane passes close to the wooded crags of Nappa Scar into the recesses of Crummackdale. At ref. 772707 the road is quit for a walled track which descends to the valley bottom to cross Austwick Beck. Another track, known as White Stone Lane, is then encountered and followed on a twisting course towards the head of the dale. We are know in the midst of a tremendous limestone arena. Ahead are the cliffs and screes of Moughton Scars, our next objective but, as yet, we are too low to see mighty Ingleborough. Further north the lane veers right to climb out of the dale and terminates at a gate in a dry-stone wall. Beyond the gate a good, grassy track climbs to the

limestone pavements which form the eastern edge of Moughton Scars. The grandeur of the walk is now apparent. To the west, across the vast crusted pavements of limestone, lies Ingleborough whilst, in the opposite direction, proud Pen-y-Ghent looks equally impressive.

The route continues along the edge of the scars north-westwards before a grassy track climbs to the west of the cliffs to a small gate by a wall junction at the southern edge of Sulber (ref.776732). The bridleway from Clapham is now joined and this is followed northwards for a short way until a path from Horton is met. This leads us across the southern flanks of Simon Fell passing Sulber and Nick Pots and an old shooting hut. When the ridge is attained it is a simple stroll westwards to reach Ingleborough's expansive summit plateau.

The return route is similar to that used in the Newby Cote as far as Trow Gill and so I will describe it to this point only briefly. Aim for the cairn at the edge of the plateau east of the summit trig point. From here a distinct path descends due south to Little Ingleborough (not named on 1:50000 maps). A sketchy path then descends south eastwards over steep slopes to reach Fell Beck. The stream is followed southwards past the cavernous pothole, Gaping Gill, before veering to the south west to enter the a shallow valley which deepens and narrows into the gorge-like ravine of Trow Gill. Take care negotiating the boulders at the narrow neck of this dark gorge.

Beyond Trow Gill the Clapham route is abandoned. Instead of turning right onto Clapdale Drive, which continues to Ingleborough Cave, turn left by the dry stone wall which then bends to the right. After about 150 yards a gate in the wall

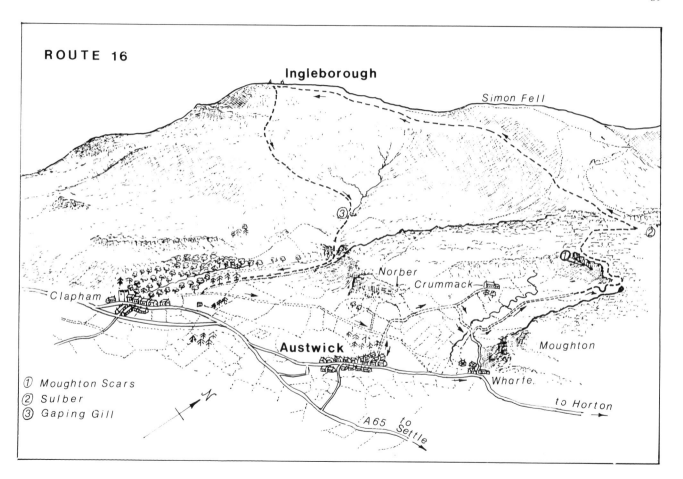

ROUTE 16

Ingleborough

Simon Fell

③

②

①

Norber
Crummack

Clapham

Austwick

Moughton

Wharfe

to Horton

A65 to Settle

N

① Moughton Scars
② Sulber
③ Gaping Gill

near sheepfolds marks the start of Long Lane. This rough walled track descends southwards beneath Thwaite Scars and offers wide and lofty views over the wooded dene of Clapham Beck and across the wide Wenning Valley to the hills of Bowland. The track terminates at Thwaite Lane, close to Clapham Lake. This is followed eastwards beneath Norber and the impressive promontory of Robin Proctor's Scar. To the south of Nappa Scars the track meets the metalled Crummack Lane used on the outward journey. A right turn along it will lead to Austwick once more.

WHERNSIDE

Whernside at 2419 feet has been Yorkshire's highest mountain since the boundary changes of 1974 removed Mickle Fell to Durham. It is a long sprawling ridge lying to the north of Ingleton and to the east of Dent. High passes connect its slopes with Simon Fell to the east and with Great Coum to the west.

The gritstone summit mass, whose ridge is known as Cable Rake, crowns a deep shelf of carboniferous limestone and its flanks are smooth and grassy with few protruding crags. The ridge is broad in its lower regions, and rises, at first in shallow gradients which then steepen and narrow towards the summit.

The Whernside Tarns lie on an almost flat gritstone shelf to the north of Cable Rake. Below them on slopes strewn with gritstone rocks are several large cairns standing prominently above steeper slopes, which then fan out to the River

Dee in beautiful Dentdale. An ancient road, known as the Craven Way, links Dent with Ribblehead, crossing the shoulder of Great Wold on these northern flanks

Whernside's steep eastern flanks decline to the sullen Greensett Tarn which is drained by Force Gill, a tumbling mountain stream with two exquisite waterfalls. Ribblehead is dominated by the huge Batty Moss Viaduct on the Settle to Carlisle Railway completed in the 1870's. There are many tales of the thousands of navvies who occupied shanty towns in the area. One thing is sure scores lost their lives and will be buried 'neath the soils of Batty Moss for they led very hard and dangerous lives.

In the west, Whernside's barren slopes decline to White Shaw Moss, a saddle of high land, separating the valleys of Deepdale and Kingsdale and also connecting it with the Great Coum -Gragareth Ridge. Southern slopes decline gradually to Scales Moor, an extensive and interesting area of limestone pavements which include fluted pot-holes and a huge example of an erratic boulder. At the eastern boundary of Scales Moor and above the lush valley of the River Doe, is Twisleton Scar whose harsh crags are well favoured by climbers. At the southern end of the ridge are the spectacular waterfalls of the Ingleton Glens formed by the River Twiss and the River Doe.

Being part of the infamous Three Peaks Walk, Whernside has had a hard life of late and the direct route used from Batty Moss via Winterscales is now horribly eroded and will take generations to recover. Other parts of the hill are quiet. Seen from the valley floor, it has neither the majesty nor

Ingleborough from Scales Mo

presence of either Ingleborough or Pen-y-Ghent but those who climb its spacious wild moorland expanses will be able to survey superior views of secluded dales, high rolling ridges and distant mountains - all adding up to a very satisfying experience.

Route 17
WHERNSIDE - a Circular from Dent

Distance 12 miles - fairly strenuous

This unspoiled lengthy approach offers the contrasting pastoral beauty of lowland Dentdale with the harsh and stark moors around the Whernside Tarns. This is crowned by the majesty of the wild Cable Rake ridge and mountain summit.

The route begins on the cobbled streets of Dent. At the crossroads in the centre of the village, the narrow road to Cowgill is followed for a few hundred yards. The bridge over the River Dee is encountered but not crossed. Here the swift flowing river's southern banks are followed through rich green meadows to its confluence with Deepdale Beck which is followed until another country lane is encountered (ref. 721861).

A few hundred yards eastwards, by an old Methodist Chapel, a right turn is made along Dark Hall Lane. A left turn at the corner of a small wood, where two large pine trees stand, leads to a stony track which climbs south-westwards over reed-covered ground. On 1:50000 maps the track which eventually leads to Ribblesdale, is marked as the course of the Dales Way but the track is correctly titled the Craven Way on 1:250000 maps.

Height is gained rapidly and the quiet beauty of secluded Deepdale is soon revealed. Ahead cairns on Whernside's shoulder stand out prominently against the sky, enticing the walker to press on. When the track levels out, temptation to abandon it, hop over the walls and head directly for the cairns should be resisted. Instead its course should be followed to the last wall corner. Here a faint path climbs southwards over the grassy moors of the Great Wold. The path deviates westwards to reach the first cairn, which stands amongst a rash of gritstone boulders. From here, Great Coum is the centre-piece

Approaching Cable Rake from the north

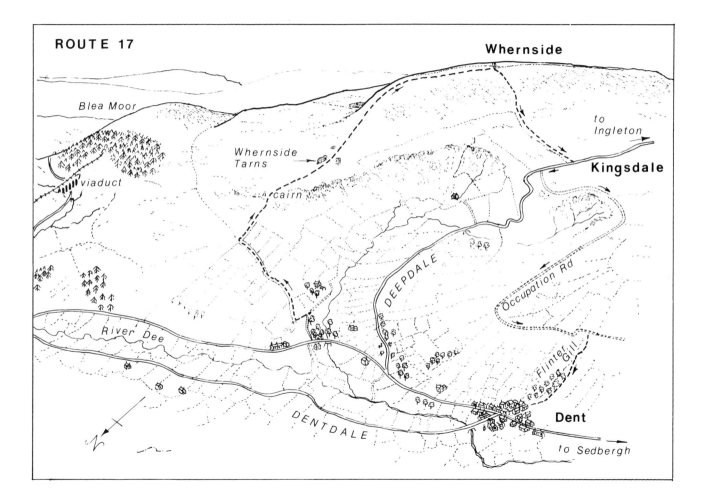

ROUTE 17

Whernside

Blea Moor

Whernside
Tarns

cairn

to
Ingleton

Kingsdale

DEEPDALE

Occupation Rd

viaduct

River Dee

Flinter Gill

Dent

DENTDALE

to Sedbergh

of a splendid hillscape to the west. The tawny slopes of this elegant colossus are accentuated by the stone walls which decline to gentler green fields of Deepdale where the River Dee can be seen meandering towards Sedbergh to join the waters of the Lune. Beyond, the smooth rounded crests of the Howgill Fells lead the eye across their northern shoulder to the more distant Lakeland Peaks.

After a short ascent, the path reaches another cairn on the edge of a shelf of level terrain. Here it passes over a natural gritstone causeway between the two largest of the Whernside Tarns. Heading due south, the view is filled with Cable Rake, the high ridge of Whernside. When the base of the ridge is reached, a new landscape to the east unfolds. Greensett Tarn lies brooding two hundred feet below the precipitous eastern escarpment of Whernside's highest ground whilst, further afield, beyond Ribblehead, Pen-y-Ghent sits proudly on the skyline.

The final ascent begins and the wall that straddles southwards over the mountain is followed to the summit, just over half a mile distant. Here panoramas of the plains of Lancashire, the Bowland Fells and the superb spectacle of Ingleborough are added to the list of impressive vistas offered on this route. The sighting of York Minster is also possible. This has been proven by the flashing of lights between the two, though I suggest this feat required the use of a powerful telescope!

The descent is by means of a lightly used route which declines directly westwards to White Shaw Moss, Kingsdale. Here the Ingleton to Dent road straddles the moors between Whernside and Great Coum. The road is followed northwards until, at ref. 723823 a left turn is made along a walled track known locally as the the Occupation Road but named on maps as Green Lane. The rutted track circumvents the combe of Gastack Beck beneath the slopes of Green Hill and Great Coum. It is followed to its junction with the Flinter Gill Track, Ref.698858. which descends by the pleasant limestone ravine back to Dent. (see routes to Great Coum for more detail)

Route 18
WHERNSIDE from Ribblehead

Distance 8 miles - moderate

This route traverses desolate moors and mosses to the east of the summit. Now they are empty but, once upon a time, they would have been teeming with navvies who worked on the construction of the Settle to Carlisle Railway conveyed here by the famous Batty Moss (sometimes known as Ribblehead) Viaduct.

North of the Railway Inn, Ribblehead, (ref. 765793) a wide track leaves the road to cross the open spaces of Batty Moss. Whernside's whaleback escarpment forms the backdrop to the huge stone-built Victorian viaduct whose arches number twenty-four in all and each a hundred foot high.

On reaching the viaduct, try looking to the south where the giant archways frame a lovely vista of Ingleborough. The path stays close to the course of the railway, passing the isolated signal box at Blea Moor, where the signalman enjoys an enviable view of the three peaks. The line is crossed by a

Striding northwards over Cable Rake with the frozen Greensett Tarn below

77

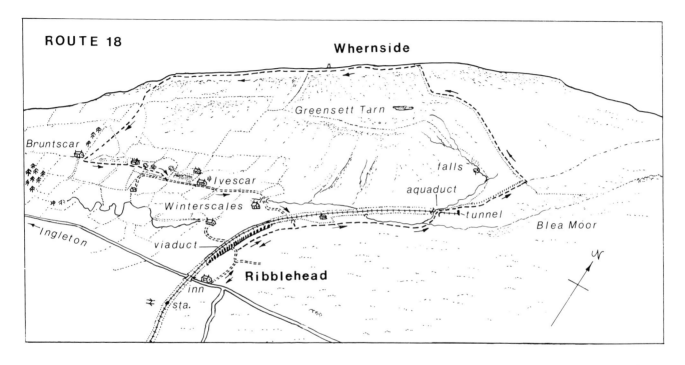

ROUTE 18

Whernside

Greensett Tarn

Bruntscar

Ilvescar

Winterscales

falls

aquaduct

tunnel

Blea Moor

Ingleton

viaduct

Ribblehead

inn

sta.

bridge which also carries the ensuing waters of Force Gill. A short way upstream is a waterfall which cascades fifty feet to a small amphitheatre enclosed by sheer cliffs. After this detour, steps must be retraced to recommence the route which ascends the slopes north of Force Gill using a bridleway. This follows a fence until it meets a dry-stone wall marking the Cumbria/North Yorkshire boundaries (ref.756827). The going is tough as the fence is traced westwards over quite wet and muddy terrain. The main ridge is gained to the south of Whernside Tarns.

Changing direction to head due south, the path now hugs the edge of the mountain's eastern escarpment. The steep bare slopes plunge to the moorland shelf where the dark and moody waters of Greensett Tarn lie. On the final approaches to to the summit a view of Ingleborough gradually unfolds, its rocky flanks rising majestically from the great limestone scars above Twistleton and Chapel-le-Dale.

From Whernside's summit, the panoramas are wide and contrasting. To the south, beyond the broad valley of the River Wenning, are the rolling moors of Bowland, where, in late summer, large areas are splashed with the vivid purple of flowering heather. Gragareth rises from the south-west over lonely Kingsdale and to the west across Deepdale is Great Coum, whose north facing combe is clearly visible high above the fields of Dentdale. In retrospective views, our route to the top can be clearly traced back to Ribblehead. The Settle to

Whernside from Scales Moor

Carlisle Railway line can be seen winding around the base of Simon Fell, climbing the gradient known as 'the Big Hump' before crossing Batty Moss Viaduct and disappearing into the Blea Moor Tunnel.

The direct descent eastwards from the summit is now frowned upon due to the severe erosion caused by the 'Three Peaks' route'. Instead continue southwards along the ridge to ref.735803. A path from here deviates SSE to enter the enclosed farmland which is traversed crossing stiles to reach Bruntscar Farm. Behind the farm is a cave, which tunnels for a third of a mile into Whernside. It can be viewed with permission from the farmer.

Beyond a gate to the left, a signposted bridleway is followed across fields passing Broadrake Farm to reach a track at Ivescar. This leads to Winterscales Farm and the railway at Bleamoor Sidings. After passing under the tunnel the line of the railway is followed back to Ribblehead.

Route 19
WHERNSIDE from Twisleton Scar End

Distance 12 miles (return route) - strenuous

This classic approach climbs along the crest of this great whaleback hill. Although long, it is a fine route - one of the best in Three Peaks country, traversing outstanding limestone scenery and the freedom of tranquil moorland.

The walk begins from a conveniently sited lay-by (ref. 692759) on the Kingsdale Road, two miles north of Ingleton.

A short way north, a right turn is made on a walled track which crosses the River Twiss before arriving at the foot of Twisleton Scar End. The route now ascends lush green slopes offering elevated views of Ingleton and its surrounding pastures. Beyond the edge of the scars an extensive area of limestone is entered. Hawthorns eke out an existence amongst the clints. Gnarled, twisted and windblown, they lean northwards at crazy angles.

The path continues north eastwards over the scars to Ewes Top and passes a fluted pot-hole. Beyond it our route deviates to follow the dry-stone wall which adds a definitive spine to the broad, grassy summit ridge. It is a dependable guide to the summit and also provides shelter from westerly winds. Views of Gragareth to the west across Kingsdale are completely upstaged by those to the south east. Here amongst the expanse of limestone clints stands an enormous perched boulder. Beyond it is the distinctive towering form of Ingleborough.

The limestone is left behind as climbing begins on Rigg Side. This is quiet country. The only sounds are the rustle of moorland grass underfoot and the spiralling tunes of the skylark. Few folk will be encountered on this section of the walk. A dark, peaty pool is passed on West Fell and a mile further on the ridge steepens and the final pull begins. Low Pike and then High Pike precede the top at Cable Rake. A narrow gap allows access to the summit trig point on the opposite side of the wall.

I personally feel that it is best to return to Kingsdale using the same route for the subtle changes in light will offer new perspectives and the false summits of the ascent will be

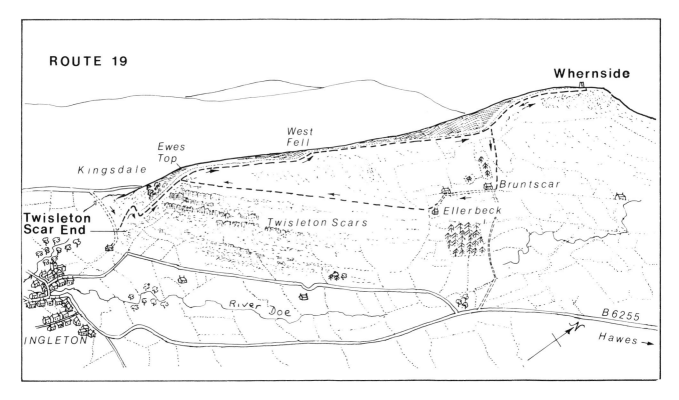

ROUTE 19

Whernside

West Fell

Ewes Top

Kingsdale

Bruntscar

Ellerbeck

Twisleton Scar End

Twisleton Scars

INGLETON

River Doe

B 6255

Hawes →

replaced by superb southern panoramas. However an alternative route does exist. Retrace the route of ascent to Low Pike where a southerly descent is made to Bruntscar Farm (see Ribblehead route for description). From here a farm road leads to Ellerbeck.

After going southwards from this second farm with a wall to the left, a gate marks the start of a bridleway which continues south westwards gradually climbing above the scars of Scales Moor to meet the main route on Ewes Top.

Facing page: Whernside and the Perched Boulder, Scales Moor
Overleaf: On Whernside's summit looking across to Ingleborough

PEN-Y-GHENT

Pen-y-Ghent means 'Hill of the Winds' and many who have dwelt on the exposed summit plateau on less than perfect days will probably think the description is very apt. Although the smallest of the 'Three Peaks' it is probably the most loved and owes this to its very distinctive outlines which dominate the surrounding landscape.

The mountain is the culmination of a broad whaleback ridge stretching between Stainforth in Ribblesdale and Halton Gill in quiet and luscious Littondale. The smooth curves of the ridge are rudely interrupted by the underlying layers of limestone and millstone grit which surface to reveal splintered crags on all but the northern flanks. South eastern slopes decline to rough moorland abutted by the featureless flanks of Fountains Fell. This moorland is rent by the sparsely populated valleys of Silverdale and Pen-y-Ghent Gill, both pleasantly decorated with limestone scars and linked by a tenuous single-track lane. Just to the north of the lane on the highest ground is Dale Head Farm which was once an old pack-horse inn. Two miles north east, near to Pen-y-Ghent House, are the remains of Neolithic burial chambers known as the Giant's Grave. Most of the stones used to enclose the tumulus have long since been removed for the area's limestone walls, however and the site is now rather obscure.

To the north of Pen-y-Ghent is Plover Hill, a high rounded peak which lies at the head of desolate terrain in which seemingly endless moorland undulates to the extremities of Wensleydale. The monotony of the landscape is only briefly interrupted by the ravines formed by the Foxup and Cosh Becks and high Langstrothdale. This is wild country in the true sense of the word.

The western side of the hill is perhaps the finest. It certainly includes the most features. A walk along the green lane north eastwards from Horton in Ribblesdale threads through beautiful areas of classic limestone topography revealing a dry valley and two spectacular chasms, the Hunt and Hull Pots. There is also a splendid continuation of the walk along the deserted moorlands of Foxup to Halton Gill in Littondale .

Route 20
PEN-Y-GHENT - a circular from Horton in Ribblesdale

Distance 5 miles - moderate

Horton is a village pleasantly situated on the banks of the River Ribble in the shadow of Pen-y-Ghent's precipitous western flanks. It is the starting point of the two of the most popular routes to the famous summit and in this description I have combined them in a circular route.

The trek begins from the lovely old parish church across whose yard a splendid prospect of the hill can be seen. A narrow lane (ref.811721) is followed to the hamlet of Brackenbottom. Here a well waymarked route climbs north eastwards across verdant pastureland with a dry-stone wall on the left acting as an infallible guide. Views of Pen-y-Ghent are limited to teasing glimpses of its dark craggy gritstone cap which peeps above the lower grassy slopes.

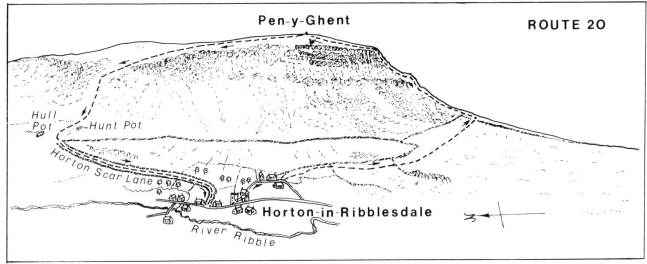

Pen-y-Ghent

ROUTE 20

Hull Pot
Hunt Pot

Horton Scar Lane

Horton-in-Ribblesdale

River Ribble

As height is gained views to the south become more expansive. The course of the River Ribble can be traced through the Craven Limestone scenery to Settle where the wider plains lead the eye to the distinctive lone escarpment of Pendle Hill. Not all that the eye surveys is pleasing however. In retrospective western views, a huge chunk of the Moughton Scars has been devoured by the vast and ugly Horton Quarry where man and his huge machines have created a festering sore on the back of a wonderful landscape of limestone crag and outcrop.

An area of exposed crags (Brackenbottom Scar) mark the transition to the rough, undulating moorland where boggy sections have been bridged by wooden duckboards in an attempt to reduce the effects of erosion. The peak's magnificent craggy western aspect is now in full view and one's head is raised high to admire that strikingly individual form which makes it easy to forgive the path makers' unsubtle constructions. On reaching the ridge (ref.836728) a high stone wall is scaled. The path climbs northwards and a scramble on the fell's precipitous southern ramparts follows in a splendid and airy finale to the summit.

Pen-y-Ghent's summit, marked by a trig point and pile of stones, is not a spectacular place but views from it are fairly wide and interesting. They include Ingleborough and Simon

Pen-y-Ghent from near Horton Scar Lane

Fell, towering above the vast Moughton Scars. To their north across Ribblehead the great whaleback escarpment of Whernside rises obscuring the Lakeland mountains. The fells of Great Knoutberry, Dodd, and more distant still, Baugh, Wild Boar and Great Shunner complete the northern panoramas. In the opposite direction Fountain's Fell, being so close, dominates but further afield across the Ribble Valley are the smooth-sloped Bowland peaks and the more isolated escarpment of Pendle Hill.

The descent is that used by Pennine Way. It crosses the summit wall before following a well defined path which traces the craggy western edge of the plateau before declining westwards by some prominent gritstone outcrops to the expansive and marshy open moorland below. Another path leads north-westwards to Horton Moor but this should be ignored - it is the one used by the Three Peaks Walk. Our path passes close to the spine chilling Hunt Pot (ref 827740), which due to the lie of the land, can easily be missed. Here a small stream spills over the abrupt edge of an eliptical chasm whose modest aperture dimensions are completely overshadowed by its fearsome invisible depths.

A small detour is needed to visit the equally impressive Hull Pot. This can be found by following the grassy track extending northwards beyond the Horton Scar Lane (one of those famous Yorkshire Green Lanes). Hull Pot resembles the depression of a giant footstep, nearly 300 feet long, by 60 feet wide and 60 feet deep. It is best seen after periods of high rainfall when a stream, which is normally subterranean, surfaces and cascades over the craggy northern face.

Hull Pot

To return to Horton, steps should be retraced to the green lane which is then followed south westwards alongside a dry valley. It is an attractive stroll and fitting finale to a superb walk. On fine summer evenings the impressive western face of Pen-y-Ghent should be embellished by the last rays of the setting sun.

Route 21
PEN-Y-GHENT from Foxup

Distance 11 miles (circular) - moderate

This northern approach to Pen-y-Ghent is the longest described and, although not as spectacular as the more famous Dale Head and Horton routes, it is free from their crowds and the scars of erosion. Foxup, which means valley of the foxes, is a secluded hamlet bathed in silence. It lies by the confluence of the Cosh and Foxup becks. From here the watercourse becomes the River Skirfare which flows through beautiful Littondale.

The walk has a delightful start climbing the eastern slopes of Plover Hill on the old Foxup Road which begins at ref.872767 opposite to Bridge Farm. As height is gained the pleasing patterns of limestone walls accentuate the shapely and verdant hills forming the backdrop to the hamlet. On Far Bergh the track passes through an area of outcrop and shakeholes on a westward course parallel to Foxup Beck. We are now in the midst of a wild, wide landscape whose silence is broken rarely and then only by the shrill sounds of the plover, curlew or lark. Provided that the atmosphere is clear the view ahead will be enlivened hereabouts by the appearance of the distinctive flat-topped profile of Ingleborough

On Foxup Moor, ref.846762, the old road is left for a right of way which climbs southwards up the steep flanks of

Plover Hill heading for a prominent group of splintered limestone crags. The route passes to the west of the crags to reach the edge of the wide moorland plateau where there is a cluster of huge gritstone boulders which have been weathered by the elements into fine natural sculptures. Here is a good place to dwell and gaze upon a northern hillscape which includes wave upon wave of rolling, barren uplands encompassing Langstrathdale, Dodd Fell and Baugh Fell and on the distant horizon, the bulky Great Shunner Fell.

A series of wooden marker posts act as a guide over the peaty terrain of the plateau to Plover Hill's zenith. From here

Brackenbottom Farm, Horton

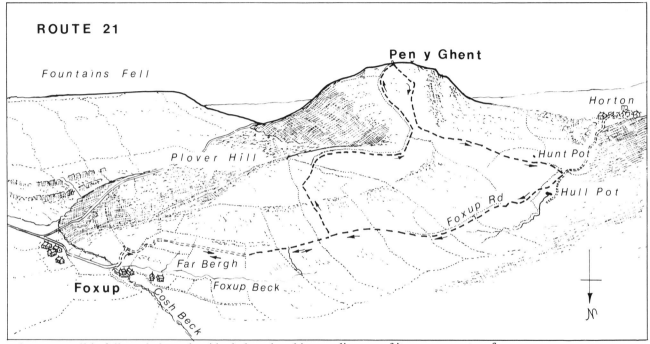

ROUTE 21

Fountains Fell

Pen y Ghent

Horton

Plover Hill

Hunt Pot

Hull Pot

Foxup Rd

Far Bergh

Foxup Beck

Foxup

Cosh Beck

N

a drystone wall is followed along the ridge's broad arching back towards Pen-y-Ghent. In the prospect to the west, Ingleborough is now in full view, rising above the limestone pavements of Sulber and Fell Close. The bulky form of Fountain's Fell fills the southern scene across Silverdale. Ahead the true character of Pen-y-Ghent is largely obscured from this vantage but there is a hint of its nobility in brief glimpses of its craggy eastern face.

A final assault over steep grassy slopes leads to the summit (and the crowds) where there are rewards of the expansive panoramas which a have previously been obscured by the hill itself.

The return route descends Pen-y-Ghent's western flanks past Hunt Pot to the shooting hut at the head of the Horton Scar

Lane (see Horton route). A right turn (NE) is then made on the old Foxup Road which passes to the east of Hull Pot then close to some grouse butts before traversing Horton Moor. The track rounds Plover Hill to meet the outward path on Foxup Moor at ref. 846762. Steps are then retraced to Foxup to complete the trip.

Route 22
PEN-Y-GHENT from Dale Head

Distance 2 miles (one way) - fairly easy

The spectacle from Dale Head of the dawn sun's first piercing rays across Pen-y-Ghent is indelibly etched on my mind and I have often watched the spectacle begin with a spark of gold glinting across the summit before growing and slowly rolling back the shadows of the night. Pennine Way travellers will be familiar with this easy route, which involves less than nine hundred feet of ascent. It begins on the high moors above Silverdale between Pen-y-Ghent and Fountains Fell. .

A track leaves the Stainforth to Halton Gill road at ref.842714 passing through an area of limestone outcrop preceding the pleasantly situated rustic farm of Dale Head. Beyond the farm, a delightful path climbs towards the ridge to the south of the main summit massif. Here the uninteresting Churn Milk Hole is reached and a track turns to the north heading directly for Pen-y-Ghent, whose finest aspect is now seen. This favoured fell appears a colossus with its twin steps of millstone grit and limestone emphasised by the plain backcloth of rough empty moorland - a riveting sight. The expansive moors which decline to Brackenbottom in the west and Pen-y-Ghent Gill to the east are quiet, save for the occasional calls of grouse.

On reaching the foot of the mountain's bold ramparts, the wide track becomes sketchy and plots an intricate route through the surrounding crags. This section provides most of the route's collar work with just a brief respite above the first tier of limestone. Here the gradient eases amidst a chaotic jumble of gritstone outcrop, dissected by a well constructed

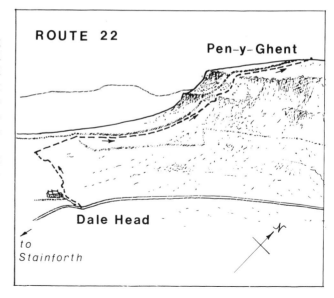

dry-stone wall. The northbound path then climbs steeply once more, threading its way amongst the second tier consisting of dark millstone grit crags. It emerges at the edge of the grassy plateau where the wall is followed to the summit.

There are no quick alternative routes back to Dale Head without having to scale dry-stone walls. A lengthy circular could be undertaken by continuing along the ridge to Plover Hill thence descending to Foxup Moor. At ref.872764, above the hamlet of Foxup, a bridleway would lead to the Halton Gill - Stainforth Lane above Pen-y-Ghent Gill. One mile further west a footpath, running parallel to the road, continues past Pen-y-Ghent House, and Giants Grave. The last mile back to Dale Head is by road and the complete walk would be ten miles.

Descending from Pen-y-Ghent's summit to Dale Head with Pendle Hill on the horizon

On the Gt. Coum Gragareth Ridge looking south to Ingleboroug

THE WESTERN PEAKS

GREAT COUM & CRAG HILL

Route 23 From Kingsdale
Route 24 From Dent via Flinter Gill,

GRAGARETH

Route 25 Horseshoe Walk
Route 26 From Keld Head

CALF TOP

Route 27 A Circular from Barbon

ADDITIONAL INFORMATION

O.S. Landranger Maps 1:50000 Nos 97 'Wensleydale & Upper Wharfedale'
and No.98 'Kendal to Morecambe': Outdoor Leisure 1:25000 Yorkshire
Dales Western Area; For Calf Top Pathfinder 1:25000 No 628 'Kirkby
Lonsdale & Barbon' is most useful.

ACCOMMODATION
The Sun (05875.256) & The George and Dragon (05875.208) in Dent; The
Red Dragon, Kirkby Lonsdale (05242.71205); The White Swan Inn, Middleton
(046836.223). Dalesman Country Inn, Sedbergh (05396.21183).
Youth Hostel; Ingleton; Cowgill (5 miles east of Dent)
Camp-sites: Dent (2) and Ingleton..

Railway Stations at Dent and Garsdale Head (Leeds - Carlisle Line) and
Bentham (Leeds - Lancaster/Morecambe Line) and Kendal.

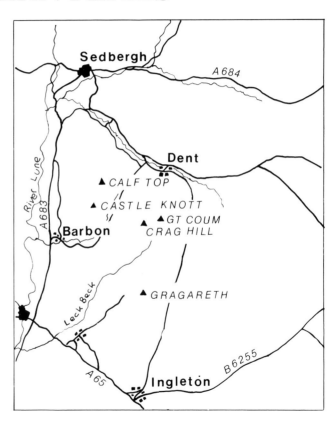

Looking across to Calf Top from the Crag, Crag Hill

GREAT COUM CRAG HILL

Great Coum and Crag Hill are closely paired summits whose rough northern flanks decline to the beautiful meadows of Dentdale. Their desolate grassy southern slopes are drained by Ease Gill, which two miles downstream sinks beneath beds of limestone in a fascinating area of pot-holes, caves and waterfalls.

The trig point on Crag Hill's summit overlooks the expansive stark western fellside which gradually descends to the wild and lonely valley of Barbondale. Half a mile to the north east lie some dark gritstone outcrops, (marked on 1:25000 maps as The Crag) crowned by a huge stone cairn.

Great Coum has intricately contoured slopes which are more appealing to the walker than Crag Hill. The mountain takes its name from the high combe which has been scooped from its north eastern flanks. The tell-tale signs of limestone geology are still evident, although not as obvious on the high fells as say, Ingleborough or Pen-y-Ghent. There are many disued small quarries and high on the eastern side, above the wild hanging valley of Gastack Beck, are the pale crags of Binks. There are also numerous examples of shake-holes and subterranean streams. Gatty Pike, furnished by a rash of boulders and huge pile of stones, is surprisingly omitted by name from the 1:50000 O.S. maps. It will be remembered for its fine views of both Whernside and Ingleborough.

Great Coum and Crag Hill are most often climbed from Dent. Here their majestic northern slopes are decorated by a collection of tall cairns known as the Megger Stones and riven by the delightful sylvan limestone ravine of Flinter Gill. I have shown three routes to the tops, one of which includes Gragareth in a grand horseshoe ridge walk of the whole range.

Route 23
GREAT COUM & CRAG HILL From Kingsdale

Distance 3¹/₂ miles (one way) 7 miles returning via the Combe - easy

The starting point for this route lies at ref. 723823, nearly five miles south of Dent and where the narrow Ingleton Road winds up the high moorland between Gragareth and Whernside. Here, on the fifteen hundred foot pass at the head of Deepdale and Kingsdale, a walled 'green lane' leads westwards past disued quarries at High Pike and towards the whaleback grassy escarpment which culminates at Great Coum. Beyond the quarries the track traverses Foul Moss. It becomes marshy in places, especially where it veers northwards at the head of Gastack Beck. Views have been improving as if to compensate for the lack of firm terrain. Ingleborough has risen from the southern horizon. Its distinctive and unmistakable profile completely overshadows the featureless flanks of its nearer neighbour, Whernside. In turn, Whernside dominates the low landscapes of Deepdale and Dentdale, its barren simplicity complimenting the complex field patterns of their verdant vales.

A gate in the wall (706825) provides access to the grassy fellsides between Green Hill and Great Coum. Here the collar work begins on a steep, trackless westerly course to the ridge which is gained near to the County Stone marking the borders of Lancashire and North Yorkshire. Crag Hill is seen for the first time across the wild upper valley of Ease Gill. By looking south westwards down the valley, the rounded hills of Bowland can be seen beyond Lancaster and Morecambe Bay.

The climb northwards is fairly easy - a typical pleasant ridge walk, in fact. The first landmark is Gatty Pike and marked by a huge pyramidal cairn perched on a rash of crag and boulder. From here the view across the scarred sides of Green Hill to Ingleborough is riveting but, before the great northern vistas appear, the final approach to Great Coum must be made!

There are no great cairns, shelters - not even one of those concrete triangulation points to mark the highest place (you even have to scale a dry-stone wall to get there). This detracts little for all the attentions will be focussed on the wide-sweeping views of Calf Top, the Howgill Fells and, on a good day the Lakeland Fells - High Street being most prominent. This is a spacious perch and probably it will be all yours!

A line of tall cairns along the north side of the ridge wall lead to The Crag (only marked on 1:25000 maps) situated a quarter of a mile north-east of Crag Hill's summit. The position is ideal for a lunch stop. The outcrops are gritstone and perched upon them is a tall stone cairn overlooking the valley of Barbondale. From the depths of the valley rise the strangely uniform steep sides of Barkin, whose summit is better known as Calf Top. The uniformity is eccentuated by the stone walls which run parallel from ridge to valley, dividing the fellsides into equal vertical portions.

A south westerly course for three hundred yards will lead to the ridge wall close to Crag Hill's summit, which is marked by a trig. point. Although less dramatic than The Crag, the views from the top are wider and include one across Ease Gill and Gragareth to Whernside and Ingleborough.

Variations on a return route are limited to a detour on the southern arm of Great Coum to meet the Green Lane at ref.

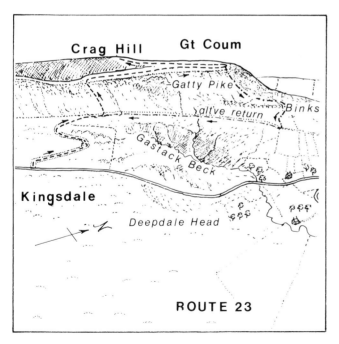

ROUTE 23

712836. This would give good views of the Gastack Beck Waterfalls and of course the combe itself.

Route 24
GREAT COUM & CRAG HILL from Dent via Flinter Gill

Distance 7 miles - moderate

Dent, one of Yorkshire's pleasantest villages, has narrow cobbled streets and lies by the River Dee. It is surrounded by green meadows which soar in graceful sweeps to the high moors of Great Coum and Rise Hill.

The walk to Great Coum's summit commences from the ample car park. A narrow lane opposite leads southwards past some picturesque cottages towards Flinter Gill, a wooded limestone ravine. A wide, well used stony track skirts the western edge of the gill which is obscured in most places by the profuse woodlands lining its precipitous sides. The boisterous stream echoes in the dark and confined depths.

On reaching the open fellsides, considerable interest is aroused by the wide vistas which include Calf Top across wild Barbondale, the Howgills beyond lower Dentdale and Dent dwarfed by Rise Hill. Flinter Gill is now shallow-banked and its stream flows playfully on a meandering course through pale grasslands with the odd twisted Rowan punctuating the scene. At ref. 698858 the track joins Green Lane (known locally as the Occupation Road), an ancient road linking Barbondale and Deepdale. This is followed south eastwards for just under a mile. It is then abandoned for a route to the

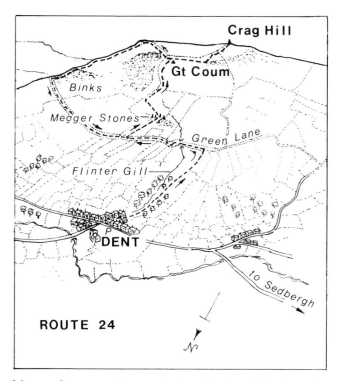

ROUTE 24

Megger Stones, a strange cluster of cairns built from the abundant local limestone. The way begins at a gate (ref. 706854) in the wall to the right of the track a short way after passing a tree and ruin on the same side. The Megger Stones will be seen on the horizon to the south west. Their lofty

On Crag Hill looking across Dentdale to the Howgill Fells

position offers superb views down the length of Dentdale, and the surrounding fells of Whernside, Great Shunner, Widdale, and Baugh can now be clearly seen.

From here a way is forged directly to Great Coum's summit. This is done by climbing to a wall corner. The wall to be followed now leads southwards bending south westwards to the summit. One wall will have to be scaled, an easy prospect but do take care not to cause any damage!.

To descend, the combe itself is circumvented on steep grassy slopes down to the quarry and limestone crags of Binks. A track from the quarry then leads back to the Green Lane Track. From here there are views of the cavernous corrie where Gastack Beck, a spout-like waterfall, cascades over mossy crags and steep grassy slopes into Deepdale. Green Lane is now followed back to the top of Flinter Gill giving splendid ever-changing views of Dentdale en route. Steps are retraced by Flinter Gill back to Dent.

GRAGARETH

Gragareth is the south eastern outlier of the horse-shoe of high fells which culminate at Great Coum. Situated four miles north of Ingleton, this expansive grassy eminence is built on a plinth of limestone and very much in the mould of its more famous neighbour, Whernside which lies to the east across Kingsdale.

The huge stone cairns known as the Three Men of Gragareth are the most notable features. They stand sentry high on the hill's western slopes above Leck Fell Beck, an area of limestone caves and potholes. Gragareth shows its best face proudly above Kingsdale. Striking limestone bluffs and crags vie for attention at every turn. On the approach by road from Ingleton the bold buttresses of Hunt's Cross and Tow Scar form an impressive front to the extensive terraces of Keld Head Scar, which rise steeply from Kingsdale Beck and the narrow tarmac ribbon that constitutes the Ingleton to Dent road. Above these terraces lie a series of potholes and caves including the renowned Rowten Pot which is an entrance to a dark underworld of subterranean passages and caverns.

Gragareth's summit ridge is expansive, wet in places, and grassy. It could hardly be labelled as a place of fine mountain architecture and immediate interest. Those who visit it on a less than perfect day may not bother to return for this hill's main attraction is in its wide open spaces and panoramas of the Lakeland and Yorkshire Peaks. Those who visit a day when the sun shines and the atmosphere is crystal clear will see some of the finest views in West Yorkshire and feel the freedom of wide open spaces and bracing air.

Route 25
THE GREAT COUM - GRAGARETH HORSESHOE - from Leck Fell House

Distance 10 miles moderate to hard

Encompassing the three fells of Gragareth, Great Coum and Crag Hill, this is a fine ridge walk across terrain which lends itself to a free-striding carefree gait. It offers wide panoramas of Cumbria the Lancashire Coast and West Yorkshire and also

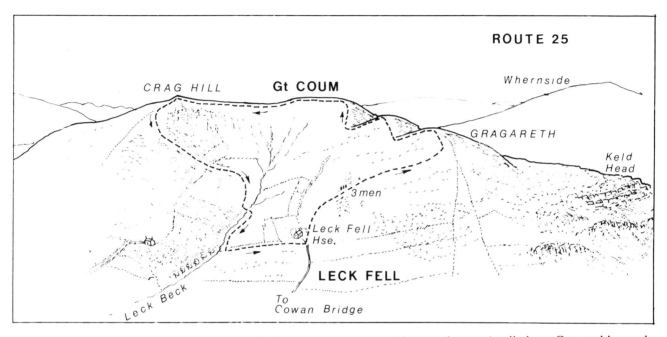

ROUTE 25

CRAG HILL Gt COUM Whernside

GRAGARETH

Keld Head

3 men

Leck Fell Hse.

LECK FELL

Leck Beck

To Cowan Bridge

generates extra interest in the final stages when the limestone cave and river scenery of Ease Gill and Leck Beck are visited.

Leck Fell House, a stark stone-built farmhouse, stands defiant of the harsh mountain elements fourteen-hundred feet high on the flanks of Gragareth. Its link with civilisation is the long tarmac lane leading to Cowan Bridge on the A65 highway. A car park (ref. 675791) at its termination on Leck Fell is handily placed for the start of the walk. A gate marks the start of the trackless north easterly climb on Gragareth's rough craggy slopes. This bold course soon leads to the trio of high cairns, the Three Men of Gragareth. They make an excellent foreground for a superb view across Crag Hill and Calf Top to the High Street Range of Lakeland. After a further four hundred feet of climbing, the peaty ridge is attained and eastern vistas of Ingleborough, Whernside are added to the panoramas. Gragareth's summit, marked by a concrete trig.

point, lies due east and is soon reached but few will tarry here for it is relatively dull and there will probably be a strong urge to stride forth northwards along the ridge.

The next peak is Green Hill, where the contrasting fertile recesses of Deepdale and Dentdale come into view. To the north of Green Hill is the county stone marking the boundaries of Lancashire and Yorkshire.

The route between the County Stone and Crag Hill are described in detail in the Kingsdale route to Great Coum. This involves a simple undulating ridge walk passing the cairn and crags on Gatty Pike before reaching Great Coum's summit. Here the ridge wall turns westwards and is followed to the second summit at Crag Hill, marked by a trig. point.

The appearance of the Howgill Fells and the Rawthey Valley from the Great Coum are a memorable feature of this walk. It will be with regret that these views are left behind when the descent has to be made from Crag Hill's summit into the seemingly dull depths of Ease Gill's valley. This is done on a rutted track which becomes indistinct beyond a derelict stone wall half way down the fellside. There are no obstacles to progress however between here and the riverbanks which are then followed downstream. As further descent is made the valley becomes more ravine-like and potholes, crags and crevices can be seen in its sides. (Bullpot Farm, nearby is a caving' and potholing centre) A wooden bridge at ref. 675805 is used to cross to the southern banks of the stream which has eroded its rockbed into strange smoothed sculptures that would have made Henry Moore proud. Slightly downstream the path passes close to Cow Holes, (not marked on maps). Here the waters tumble into a dark narrow cavern to a deep pool below. The falls, partially obscured by trees, can be seen by using a slight detour to the right of the path (well used and obvious).

A sketchy track climbs out of the picturesque craggy tree-lined ravine. By a stone wall at ref. 664802, the best course is to ascend the heather-clad sides of Leck Fell in a south easterly direction to reach, once more the car park at journey's end.

N.B.

It is possible for strong walkers to extend this horse-shoe walk by starting from Cowan Bridge (ref. 636766) and following the pleasant Leck Fell Road to Leck Fell House. On the return leg from Ease Gill there is a lovely riverside walk passing the waterfalls and caves of Leck Beck and the sylvan scenes of Spring Wood before emerging by Leck Mill. (645771) From here it is half a mile by the lane to Cowan Bridge.

Route 26
GRAGARETH From Keld Head via the Turbary Road

Distance 4¹/₂ miles (one way) or 8 miles with return via Ireby Fell - moderate (stiff climb at end)

This route, by far the most interesting ascent of Gragareth, visits examples of most major features associated with limestone geology, i.e. potholes, caves underground streams which gurgle to the surface from 'nowhere' and vast scarred white cliffs. It utilises the Turbary Road, an ancient highway

The Three Men of Gragareth

once used by locals exercising their 'Turbary Rights' - the right to cut peat from the fell for use as a fuel.

On my first acquaintance with the area I chose an afternoon when the fickle September sun more often than not favoured the peaks of Ingleborough and Whernside. The trip was memorable for the moments when it did decide to break through emblazoning and bleaching the limestone cliffs. It was also memorable for the multitudes of scurrying rabbits seen at play.

The route commences at ref. 692758 on the Ingleton-Dent road. The stony Turbary Road begins on its western side beyond a five-bar gate and passes an old lime kiln before zig-zagging up grassy slopes to the north of the shapely limestone buttresses of Hunt's Cross. Retrospective views of Ingleborough are eyecatching, although slightly marred by the unsightly quarrying scars at its foot. In views northwards the giant terraces of Keld Head Scar make a majestic foreground for Whernside whose whaleback form rises gradually from the limestone cliffs at Twistleton.

After passing through a second gate, the old road threads between the heights of Low Plain and Tow Scar, the former being easily recognised by its crowning concrete trig point. The huge boulder seen at the eastern end of Low Plain is known as The Cheese Press Stone. It weighs fifteen tons, is nine feet high and was almost certainly stranded on its perch by the movement of glaciers during the last ice-age.

North of Tow Scar, the path twists eastwards and then northwards to rise out of shallow limestone canyon avoiding the summit of North End Scar. Views across the wide plains of the River Greta to Morecambe Bay and the Bowland Hills are seen to good vantage. We have now emerged on the wide area of pavements and above Keld Head Scar. After traversing a field scattered with small clints and littered with thistles, a more distinct cart track, which has climbed from Masongill, is reached. This leads us north eastwards past a succession of sink-holes and filled in potholes. Initially it veers away from Gragareth, whose bouldery southern breast rises uninvitingly from this location.

After nearing the pavement's edge above Kingsdale, the track passes the finest pothole en route - that is Rowten Pot, a large tree fringed chasm sinking three hundred and sixty five feet below the surface to reach a network of passages and caves. It was first descended, incidentally in 1897. Five hundred yards beyond Rowten the track, now more stony, climbs due north on rougher reed-covered peaty slopes until terminating at ref. 701791. From here a bold course is taken north westwards up the steep flanks of Gragareth's eastern facade. The path varies from sketchy to non-existent in its lower reaches but a stone wall acts as an infallible guide in all conditions. The spongy terrain, so demanding of the calf muscles, gives way to steep gritstone upper slopes and natural 'steps' make the climb easier. Looking northwards along the scarred slopes of Gragareth towards Green Hill, the eye is led to the fields of Dentdale and beyond to Rise Hill. Over Ingleborough's shoulder another distinctive profile appears - that of Pen-y-Ghent. It assumes grander form as height is gained.

Gragareth's ridge is expansive, shutting out views of neighbouring valleys, but it is a very airy place giving wide open panoramas in all directions except northwards. In this direction they are obscured by the loftier peaks of Great Coum and Crag Hill. For those who want to visit the trig. point, cross the stile over the tall ridge wall and make a south westerly course across the peaty plateau.

When I did this route for the first time I varied the return by descending westwards to see the Three Men of Gragareth in the late sunlight and then went southwards across Leck Fell to rejoin the Turbary Road near North End Scar. Although it did mean crossing two walls and some rough terrain it was a very worthwhile detour.

Another possibility would be to descend via the border/ridge wall. To reduce the amount of cross walls which will

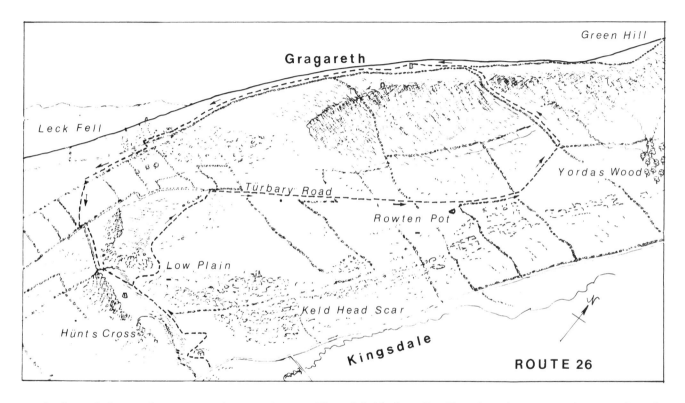

Green Hill

Gragareth

Leck Fell

Yordas Wood

Turbary Road

Rowten Pot

Low Plain

Keld Head Scar

Hunts Cross

Kingsdale

ROUTE 26

need to be scaled, enter the narrow enclosure to its west. The best place to do this is at ref. 683782 (preceding the second cross wall) for here the barbed wire along the wall top ends. At ref. 676773 a path beyond a gate to the right is followed to Marble Steps Pot. From here the route continues southwards to the right hand corner of the meadow where another gate leads to Masongill Fell Lane. A few yards further, beyond a gate, the lane becomes unenclosed and a right turn is made by a wall (R) skirting North End Scar's western ramparts. By maintaining direction at the next wall corner the track used on the outward journey will be encountered close to Tow Scar and will lead back into Kingsdale via Hunt's Cross.

Rowten Pot

CALF TOP AND CASTLE KNOTT

Calf Top is the grassy zenith of a high ridge to the west of Barbondale and to the east of the Lune Valley. It fails by one foot to reach the 2000 foot figure necessary to give true mountain status. This mathematical failure has in fact kept the mountain free from the peak baggers and thus free from erosion. The range as a whole is un-named. In my opinion its peaks belong to the quaint village of Barbon which lies to the south west amongst emerald pastures close to the confluence of Barbon Beck and the River Lune. For this reason I like to call them the Barbon Fells.

The range has many characters. To the east the slopes known as Barkin are straight and steep, soaring above the wild unpopulated valley of Barbondale. The uniform, scree-strewn slaty slopes are broken only by the dry stone walls which boldly rise to the ridge. To the west Luge Gill, Howe Gill, Wrestle Gill and Ashdale Gill dissect the hillsides to form a complex series of spurs and deep ravines.

Although very close to the Yorkshire limestone country, the incidences here are more sporadic and less spectacular. In fact the western edge of the Askrigg Block limestone strata, synonymous with the Dales' best known scenery, lies along the Dent Fault which follows Barbon Beck in Barbondale. Calf Top and its satellites consist mainly of slates and shales. Holme Knott, to the north of the region and Eskholme Pike to the south are of the limestone genre and both provide welcome relief from the spartan moors. Combe Scar, the finest feature of the range, overlooks the village of Gawthrop near Dent. These dark gritstone crags fringe a high combe and give the fell true mountain character whenever viewed from the fields of Dentdale.

Route 27
CALF TOP A Circular from Barbon

Distance 12 miles - fairly strenuous.

This route from Barbon presents a delightful start amongst the limestone crags and outcrops of Eskholme Pike before climbing to the high, deserted moors rising to Calf Top. Although the return involves some road walking the lanes used are pleasant and mainly quiet.

To the east of Barbon's charming Parish Church, a lane (ref. 631825), signposted ' To Barbon Manor' is followed northwards, crossing Barbon Beck which is heavily obscured by thicket and woods. As the lane bends to the north of the beck, it is abandoned for a footpath which traverses Barbon Park northwards towards Eskholme Farm, passing the eastern edge of a small plantation of mixed woodland en route. At the farmhouse the path assumes an easterly direction across a field to a gate sheltered by the canopy of a huge sycamore tree. Beyond the gate a bold assault commences on the steep limestone-cragged flanks of Eskholme Pike.

On reaching the summit, which is crowned with a small cairn, magnificent views to the west are revealed. Below, languishing peacefully amongst the hedgerows, tall trees and patchwork pastures is Barbon Village. Its square-towered church stands proud amongst a cluster of cottages and scattered

Calf Top and Barbondale from Castle Knott

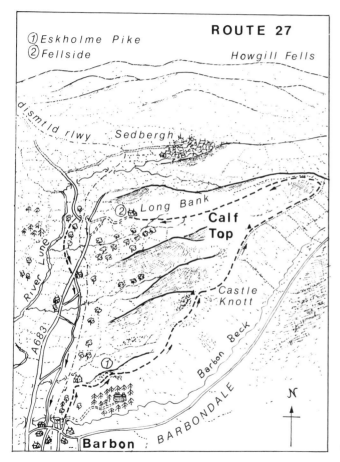

ROUTE 27

① Eskholme Pike
② Fellside

Howgill Fells

dismtld rlwy

Sedbergh

Long Bank

Calf Top

②

River Lune

A 683

Castle Knott

Barbon Beck

①

N

Barbon

BARBONDALE

farmhouses. To the east of the village and rising from the Lune Valley, Barbon Low Fell leads the eye over the small town of Kirkby Lonsdale and across the undulating farmlands surrounding Bentham and thence to the hills of Bowland, where the 'steps' of Clougha and the flat top of Ward's Stone can easily be distinguished. Further north, providing that it is a good day, we will be able to scan the Cumbrian Peaks from the Shap Fells, High Street, Helvellyn, through to the Scafells and Black Combe.

Eskholme Pike is not an easy place to leave behind on such a day but, if we are to reach Calf Top, we must first scale the swelling grassy slopes of Thorn Moor to the north east. The right of way shown on the map follows the southern edge above the conifers that surround Barbon Manor, a huge Victorian mansion built for Sir James Kay Shuttleworth, a physician from Manchester. A more direct way however is to follow the sheep-tracks along the centre of the ridge.

On reaching Castle Knott's southern spur, there is a slight change in the nature of the hills. Areas of heather can be seen on the fellside above Ashdale Gill and, in places, bouldered scars have surfaced through peaty soils. Castle Knott's summit, marked by a pile of stones, gives the first impressive views of Calf Top. The precipitous eastern slopes of Barkin plummet into the desolate valley of Barbondale along whose length, a narrow lane runs parallel to a stone-studded beck. At the head of the valley the lane drops into the more fertile lands of Dentdale which are crowded by the green slopes of Rise Hill, and the rougher ochre-tinted moors of Crag Hill .

South of Castle Knott the slopes are covered by a rash of boulders which precede a deep, soggy depression. A narrow path across the depression avoids the worst of the marshy ground but it can still be quite wet in patches as grass gives way to sphagnum moss, reeds and heather before reverting to type on the steep trackless climb up the final slopes to Calf Top. A stone wall and accompanying fence, encountered just short of the summit, run the length of the ridge northwards, and thus act as a good guide in hill fog. The summit itself is strangely barren and marked only by a concrete trig point close to a stile in the wall. In new vistas, the intricately shaped "elephant-backed" Howgill Fells form an interesting backdrop to the Rawthey Valley and town of Sedbergh. For those who wish to dwell, it is better to go over the wall and sit at the Barkin Edge where the views of Dentdale have improved to those seen from Castle Knott. Many famous Yorkshire peaks can now be spotted including Baugh Fell, Wild Boar Fell, Great Shunner, Great Knoutberry and Lovely Seat.

The route continues along the grassy ridge over Barkin Top. Crag Hill now completely obscures Ingleborough but views of Dentdale improve. The main ridge terminates at Combe Scar, an arc of glacial crags overlooking the hamlet of Gawthrop. The path veers westwards along a spur known as Long Bank which declines parallel to Dentdale into the Lune Valley. A cart track encountered, descends from the spur over the high shoulders of a heather clad moorland combe beneath Brown Knott. The change from gritstone to limestone scenery can clearly be seen in the form of Holme Knott, a shapely peak, whose trig. point is perched above pale rocky bluffs. The track fords a couple of streams before passing through the farmyard of Fellside, where a tarmac lane then leads downhill to the busy A 683 road.

After turning left along the road, a bridleway leads from the far side of the old railway bridge through woodlands by the banks of the River Lune. It meets the main road once more at ref. 624876 but this is soon abandoned for a pleasant country lane which leads southwards to Barbon.

The Lune Valley from Thorn Moor

Warrendale Knotts with Attermire Sc

THE SOUTHERN PEAKS & DALES

MALHAMDALE

Route 28 Circular from Malham

Route 29 Rye Loaf Hill-Langcliffe
  to Malham
FOUNTAINS FELL

Route 30 From Silverdale

Route 31 Circular from Tennant
  Gill

ADDITIONAL INFORMATION

O.S. Landranger Map 1:50000 No. 98 'Wensleydale & Upper Wharfedale';
O.S. Outdoor Leisure Map 1:25000 Nos 2 'Western Area' (for the Silverdale
approach to Fountains Fell) & 10 'Southern Area' (for the remaining walks)

ACCOMMODATION
The Buck Inn, Malham (07293.317), Sparth House Hotel, Malham (07293.315;
plus many hotels and guest houses at Settle including The Royal Oak
(072982.2561) & the Golden Lion (072982.2203); The Crown at Horton-in-
Ribblesdale (07296.209).
Youth Hostels at Malham, Stainforth and Horton-in-Ribblesdale.
Camp-sites at Malham, Langcliffe (nr. Settle): Stainforth and Horton-in-
Ribblesdale.

Railway Stations at Settle and Horton-in-Ribblesdale (on Settle to Carlisle
Line).

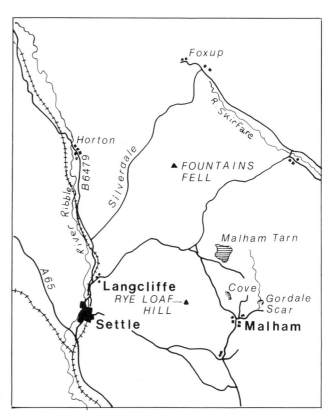

avements on the top of Malham Cove

Gordale Scar

MALHAMDALE

England's limestone scenery is never more spectacular than that of the Craven District which forms the southern part of the Yorkshire Dales. The dramatic ivory sculptures of past eons have attracted many thousands of tourists each year and include cavernous gorges, deep caves, waterfalls and streams which disappear beneath their rocky beds or tumble into dark, bottomless chasms.

Most famous features of the region are Malham Cove and Gordale Scar but if you put on your boots and walk further you will discover that the region has many other treasures.

Route 28
MALHAM COVE & GORDALE SCAR - a circular from Malham

Distance 7 miles - easy (tricky scramble at Gordale)

This is one of the classic Yorkshire Dales routes and, if you like to walk in solitude, you had better make an early start or go mid week out of the holiday periods. The popularity of the route is well deserved, for it visits some of the grandest limestone features in the whole of the British Isles.

The narrow northbound lane is followed out of the village centre until, at ref. 898633, it is left for a signposted, recently renovated stony path. This heads across fields for Malham Cove, a spectacular amphitheatre whose immense limestone cliffs were once obscured by an even more spectacular scene - that of a gigantic waterfall three times the height of Niagara. Alas Malham Beck has now permeated the porous limestone and trickles from the foot of the cliffs. It placidly flows through the verdant meadows to the right of the footpath before heading for the village. An 'improved' path climbs steeply in a series of steps to the top of the cove where there is an expansive area of limestone pavements. The grikes or channels in the pavements are often filled with plant life including hart's tongue ferns. The massive scale of the cove is evident from the top and most will dwell here. Especially dramatic is the overhanging section of crag near to the top of the 360 foot curving limestone cliff. Views to the south and west are good and include Pendle Hill, Bowland and the emerald crazed field patterns of the Ribble and Aire Valleys.

After traversing the pavements and scaling a ladder stile at their far end the route diverts NNW along a dry valley, an interesting ice-sculpted channel lined with curious crags and bluffs. At the valley head the path zig-zags below Combe Hill (not marked on 1:50000 maps) and then follows a dry-stone wall to Water Sinks where the gurgling stream from Malham Tarn goes subterranean. Beyond Water Sinks a narrow lane is encountered. After going right along it and crossing the stream the Pennine Way route is rejoined at ref. 897658. The path then goes northwards across a grassy plain to meet a wide stony track (ref.898664). Although the circular route now doubles back (south eastwards) along the track, most walkers will want to first visit Malham Tarn and its field centre. They will continue northwards to reach the eastern

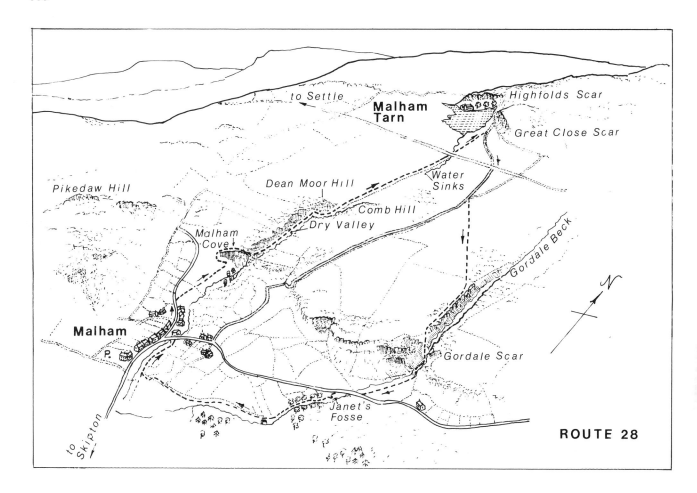

to Settle

Malham Tarn

Highfolds Scar

Great Close Scar

Pikedaw Hill

Dean Moor Hill

Water Sinks

Malham Cove

Comb Hill

Dry Valley

Gordale Beck

Malham

P.

Gordale Scar

N

Janet's Fosse

to Skipton

ROUTE 28

Malham Cove

banks of the tarn, a large lake surrounded by craggy limestone buttresses and bluffs. Malham Tarn House is set a little further north amongst delightful mixed woodland beneath the limestone cliffs of High Folds Scar. The impressive Victorian mansion was a favourite haunt of the writer Charles Kingsley, author of 'The Water Babies'. It is now owned by the National Trust and also used as a field study centre. The surrounding area is now a bird sanctuary and nature reserve.

After retracing steps to ref. 898664, the continuing wide stony track leads south eastwards to the narrow metalled Malham lane. This is followed to a stile (ref.906654) on the left hand side of the road. The right of way continues south eastwards past outcrops and clints of limestone studded with stunted hawthorns. It leads to the edge of a terraced ravine where pale cliffs stand proud over rashes of scree which line the meandering stream. The ravine's edge is traced until a stony path descends steeply into its depths. We are now above the waterfalls of Gordale Scar. The upper one is seen to pass through a window in the great cliffs which eerily close out the light. The descent to the base of the lower falls can be tricky after periods of rain and extreme caution should be exercised. A twenty foot buttress must be descended before reaching the safety of the valley floor. There are ample foot and hand-holds however and the scramble is quite exhilarating to the non-climbing fraternity.

After passing through a huge amphitheatre, a newly renovated path follows Gordale Beck into the widening pastures and thence to the road west of Gordale House Farm. Although it is possible to use the road down to Malham a better way is to make a detour to see Janet's Fosse, a pretty twenty

Victoria Cave, Langcliffe (route 29)

foot waterfall set in a sylvan glen forged by Gordale Beck. From here a riverside course leads through woods and fields down to the Pennine Way route at ref. 902625. A well trodden path then leads northwards to Malham Village.

Route 29
RYE LOAF HILL - a route from Langcliffe to Malham

Distance 6 miles - fairly easy

This route differs from others included in the book for the mountain's summit is not the culmination but a detour from the middle reaches of the trek. The route follows part of the course of an ancient road between Ribblesdale and Wharfedale. The six mile walk would be better undertaken one way only and it would be advantageous to have one car parked at either end. It could, however be part of a circular (for details see the end of the passage)

A metalled track begins from the Malham lane at ref. 830654 half a mile east of Langcliffe. After the first gate it is abandoned and the path climbs ENE across a field towards the bold limestone cliffs of Langcliffe Scar which stretch for over a mile to the Stockdale Valley. A conveniently situated ladder stile is used to scale the high stone wall which runs close and parallel to the cliffs. Slightly to the north west of the stile (a slight detour) are the Jubilee Caves, whose twin entrances are also known as Foxholes. As we look south, magnificent limestone knolls rise from the dry valley. The curiously twisted and eroded ramparts of Warrendale Knotts (west) form a deep canyon with Attermire Scar (east).

The route now heads south following the wall and passing below the huge entrance to Victoria Cave situated on a shelf with paths leading up to it. The cave, which was discovered in Coronation Year in 1838, was excavated by archaeologists. Finds included bones of species such as reindeer, the straight-tusked elephant, woolly hippo, and also the spearhead of a stone-age hunter. Many of the relics can be viewed in the Pig Yard Museum in Settle.

The descending track circumvents Attermire Scar and enters the wider plains of the Stockdale Valley. Here it meets a metalled lane which, contrary to its appearance, only has bridleway status. To the east is Stockdale Farm. The lonely farm lies dwarfed by the rounded Rye Loaf Hill which looks plain and austere by comparison to the surrounding scenery. On the northern flanks of the valley limestone crags still persist but on Rye Hill the sparse crags can be seen to consist of the darker millstone grit.

The tarmac lane is left behind to the west of the farm and a green lane continues at the foot of northern hillslopes climbing to high ground beneath Rye Hill. When co-author, Phil and I undertook the walk this part of the vale was alive with the chattering of lapwings and plovers and swarming with small rabbits scampering in earnest across the meadows.

As the Stockdale Beck veers southwards a gate in the stone wall to the right of the track is used to gain entry to the field where the final short climb up Rye Loaf's grassy flanks commences. It must be remembered that this stretch is not a right of way and care must be taken not to damage the status

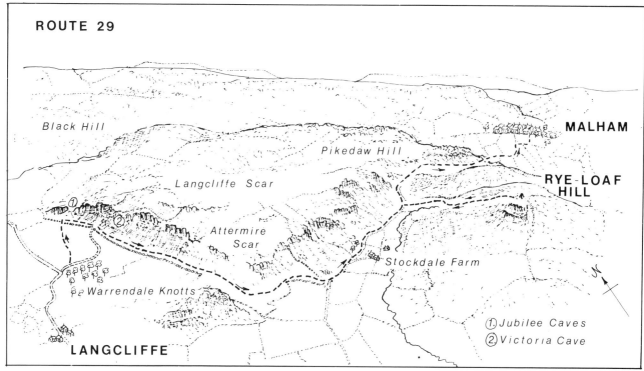

ROUTE 29

Black Hill

Pikedaw Hill

Langcliffe Scar

Attermire Scar

Warrendale Knotts

LANGCLIFFE

MALHAM

RYE-LOAF HILL

Stockdale Farm

1. Jubilee Caves
2. Victoria Cave

quo! Rye Loaf's summit is a splendid one. From its stone cairn, the panoramas southwards are only restricted by atmospheric conditions. The nearest peak is Pendle Hill, which rises in majestic isolation from the plains of the Ribble Valley. Close by are the smooth-profiled Bowland Hills and further distant across Morecambe Bay are those familiar Lakeland mountains. To the north the views are dominated by Ingleborough and Pen-y-Ghent, the latter being partially hidden by Fountains Fell. To the east the Aire Valley villages of Gargrave and Airton lie in the midst of undulating meadowland fringed by

On the summit of Rye Loaf Hill looking to Pen-y-Ghent & Ingleborough

the crags of Embsay Moor and Cracoe Fell rising above the more distant town of Skipton.

Steps must be retraced to the green lane at the head of Stockdale Beck. The eastbound journey continues, climbing to a pass to the north of Kirkby Fell, Rye Loaf's eastern neighbour. Here a junction of paths is encountered. The northerly one leads to Langscar Gate via Nappa Cross, but the one we use, continues eastwards by the clints and outcrops of Pikedaw Hill. From Pikedaw we get our first glimpses of Malhamdale, including Malham Tarn, a very pleasant sight basking by wooded slopes bordering Great Close Scar. The crazy mosaics formed by the patterns of dry-stone walls and limestone outcrops span the valley and as far as the eye can see. The first sighting of Malham Cove is eagerly anticipated but it will not appear for a while yet!

A 'Malham' sign clears the confusion at the next junction of tracks (the other leads directly to the cove). A descent is made in a shady combe lying between the contrasting limestone flanks of Pikedaw Hill and the stark gritstone crags forming Kirkby Fell's eastern face. Ahead is Malham village, many of its dwellings still obscured by the lower slopes and surrounding woodland. Malham Cove is finally seen from an old farm track used on the last approaches to the village .

Malham is huddled around a clear stream in a verdant corner to the north of Aire Head. Although popular in the daytime, it is often truly peaceful in the evening. Time it right and you could visit the magnificent cove just up the road and then eat in one of the excellent public houses or cafes!

If you want to make a circular out of this walk the best way would be to return via the cove, then northwards to Malham Tarn. From here take the lanes to Capon Hall 867667 where a right of way climbs north of Black Hill to meet the Lancliffe track at 849657.

FOUNTAINS FELL

Fountains Fell and Pen-y-Ghent boldly face each other across the upper reaches of Silverdale to the east of Settle. Unfortunately Fountains Fell does not possess the inspiring presence or magnificent architecture of its neighbour - from most angles it is a featureless grassy hill. It is however a really splendid viewpoint and offers superb vistas of all the Three Peaks!

On the northern approach from Halton Gill in Littondale, Fountains Fell reveals its finest aspect, displaying tiered terraces of limestone rising from Pen-y-Ghent Gill to the old green road, Dawson's Close. Above bare, grassy flanks rise concavely to the summit which is littered with the shafts of disused coal mines and numerous tall cairns, built. The undulating plateau is quite extensive and not a place to dwell when the cloud hangs low and thick. In a slight depression to the east of the highest land lies the lonely Fountains Fell Tarn set amongst rough moorland pasture and heather. To the south the mountain-slopes descend in a narrowing ridge to Capon Hall near Malham Tarn. A few limestone outcrops scatter the lower western hillsides on Chapel Fell and by Tennant Gill but otherwise this side of the hill is drab. Were it not for the Pennine Way it would attract few walkers. Several small stands of conifer have been planted in the regions of Darnbrook Fell.

Route 30
FOUNTAINS FELL from Silverdale

Distance 2 miles (one way) fairly easy

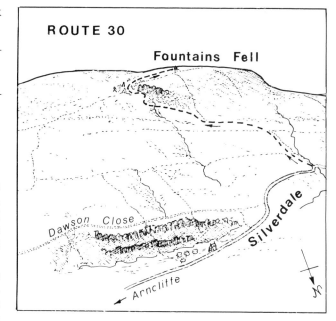

Those who just want a quick ascent to one of Yorkshire's major summits would find this route ideal. It begins at ref. 853724 on the high pass between the valleys of Silverdale and Pen-y-Ghent Gill. The pass is served by a narrow tarmac lane which links the villages of Stainforth in the Ribble Valley and Halton Gill at the head of lonely Littondale.

A sketchy track strikes south eastwards following a dry-stone wall along the grassy lower slopes of Fountains Fell. A rutted track then rakes eastwards to circumvent the northern shoulder of the fell. The upper slopes are more boulder-strewn and the path passes by dark crags which fringe the edge of the summit plateau. By this edge, a large cairn marks another change in direction. The track veers southwards to enter a complex of derelict coal mining shafts. Numerous tall stone 'men' also decorate this airy summit which offers widesweeping views including Great Whernside, Buckden Pike, Ingleborough and Pen-y-Ghent. The last mentioned is seen at its magnificent best soaring above intermediate

moorland in graceful arcs whose uniformity is broken by screes and tiered crags.

The seldom visited true summit of Fountain's Fell lies to the south west and is marked by a large cairn. It can be reached by simply following the ridge wall. The Silverdale route could be quite successfully linked to an ascent of Pen-y-Ghent in a lengthy circular trek from Foxup visiting Plover Hill en-route, and descending northwards from Fountains Fell to Dawson Close and thence to Litton. A valley path by the River Skirfare then returns to Foxup via Halton Gill.

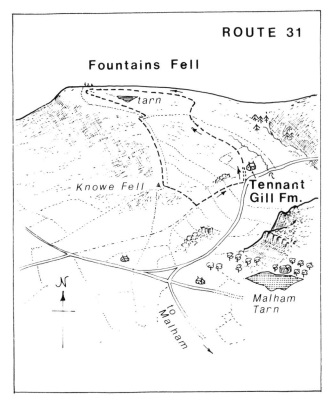

Route 31
FOUNTAINS FELL - A Circular via Tennant Gill Farm

Distance - 7 miles - moderate

The Pennine Way's southern approach to Fountains Fell is a little dull but can be vastly improved by combining it with a long but leisurely descent on the hill's southern spur before following a bridleway across Knowe Fell back to the start at Tennant Gill.

The route begins from the Stainforth to Arncliffe lane on a high wild pass at the head of the valley of Cowside Beck (ref. 884692). The drab green slopes of Fountains Fell are relieved by the limestone crags just to the west of Tennant Gill Farm, a lonely dwelling set back a couple of hundred yards from the lane. The farm's approach road is followed before continuing on a well used path which climbs generally in a north western direction to reach the ridge north east of the true summit. Several tall stone cairns surround the area which was once mined for coal. Today the deep shafts remain but, in the interests of safety, have been fenced off. The heather clad, peaty plateau to the south is quite expansive. A large tarn lies in a marshy, heather-clad depression to the south west. Its a wonderful but desolate place - ideal for those who like tranquillity.

From the area of shafts, a left turn is made by the ridge wall. This will lead south westwards to the highest ground marked by a cairn. If the weather is clear follow the wide ridge south eastwards from here to pass by the lonely tarn. After veering slightly to the right from the tarn, a slight ascent will lead to the 662 metre spot height (ref.868708). If conditions are misty follow the ridge wall southwards turning right at an intersection and left as the wall turns sharp left - otherwise descend directly south missing the dog-leg and meet the wall further down the hill. The wall leads eventually to the trig point on Knowe Fell (593m). There are really pleasant views of Malhamdale from here including Malham Tarn and the intricate surrounding limestone crags and buttresses. Leaving the minor summit, an easterly descent is assumed crossing an area of shake holes and outcrops. At ref. 877683 the vague, grassy bridleway between Henside and Tennant Gill Farm is encountered and its course traced north eastwards passing through gates and stiles in the intervening fences and walls.

On the summit plateau Fountains Fell

Winter in the Dales – a wilderness experience

BIBLIOGRAPHY

Exploring the Yorkshire Dales - Brian Lee (Countryside Publications)
The Pennine Mountains - Terry Marsh (Hodder)
Walking the Dales - Mike Harding (Michael Joseph)
Pennine Way Companion - A.W. Wainwright (Westmorland Gazette)
Walks on the Howgill Fells - A.W. Wainwright (Westmorland Gazette)
Yorkshire Dales: Ordnance Survey Leisure Guide (AA Publications)
Walks in Wensleydale - Paul Hannon (Hillside)
The Three Peaks of Yorkshire - Harry Rée & Caroline Forbes (Whittet)
Classic Walks - Richard Gilbert & Ken Wilson (Diadem)